It's **SPIRIT**, **Stupid**, **NOT** Matter

...the answer to ALL
the world's problems

Dan McAneny

Table of Contents

From the Author to the Reader

Chapters:

From the Author to the Reader

All the world's problems? Who could make such a ridiculous claim? And beyond the needless "stupid," invective what do you mean by "It's Spirit, Not Matter?" Good questions. How could you take seriously anyone who makes this claim and talks about "spirit," when we know little about "spirit" and a lot about "matter," or at least some of our scientists do.

Who am I calling stupid? These very same scientists. They certainly are not stupid about all the discoveries and inventions they're responsible for, which have made our lives so much better in so many ways. So we owe them a debt of gratitude. In fact, they are only stupid about one thing – their refusal to seriously investigate the world of consciousness and spirit, to see what benefits we might derive.

Let's cut right to the chase. Any problem you can think of is caused by our mistaken assumption that we are material creatures, physical creatures, instead of what we really are – spirits. Yes, right now as we experience time, we are spirits in human form, but we won't always be in human form, and we will always exist as spirits.

This book will briefly summarize the reasoning behind the assumption that we are all spirits, not just physical creatures. The word briefly is emphasized, because the logic and the evidence have been presented in detail in some of my previous books. You will either accept that reasoning or not.

If you accept it, or if you momentarily "suspend disbelief" and are willing to consider what our world and our daily experience would be like if all of us understood that we are spirits, you can join me in speculation about the great experiences we'd all have, and the end of all our problems. One of the sources mentioned in this book claims that many of us will begin to understand this by the year 2075, as noted in *The 2075 Movement*. It's not very far in our future, so why not get started now?

Chapter 1 - We Have a Problem

We really can't blame ourselves for paying almost all of our attention to the physical world we experience every day, largely ignoring the world of spirit. After all, that's what we came in for – to experience the physical world with all of the challenges we've set up for ourselves while we're here, and to grow in many ways through this physical experience.

But even though we can't blame ourselves, we do have a problem. We have forgotten that we are spirits! We think of ourselves mainly as physical beings. We perceive a world out there of objects and events that are separate from us. We seem to have little control over events and "things that happen to us." Unfortunately, the events that are happening to a large portion of our fellow humans don't look too promising.

You can make up your own list. You can choose from the following or make up your own. Millions of refugee families living in squalid conditions … hundreds of thousands of people killed or tortured by terrorist armies or dictators … sex trafficking … starvation and hunger …widespread disease … hatred and insults spewing forth from millions on a daily basis … weapons of war that are capable of killing millions of us quickly … and many more.

In many cases our own life might be joyful, productive and happy, filled with warm relationships. But we're still aware of all those fellow humans enduring a miserable existence. We'd like to help, we'd like all their lives to be as happy as ours, but we don't know how to do that.

Some of us might volunteer to help others, or start a company that gives meaningful employment to a lot of people, but we know we're touching just a small portion of those who need help. There are millions who need help from someone, but they're not getting it, so they continue being tortured, forced to be sex slaves, starving, suffering, living in refugee camps (Is that any way for a little girl or boy to spend their childhood?) or contracting deadly diseases. That leaves us with an uneasy feeling. Somewhere there must be a solution, we know, but we just haven't found it. There is progress in a lot of areas, but we do not see anything on the horizon that might be the answer for millions in unhappy existences.

What is the answer? It's simple … but strange to us. We just have to become aware of something we already know at some level. It is this. Despite the mountains of evidence our five senses deliver to our minds every day, we are not physical creatures. We are spirits, temporarily operating in a human physical body, for a variety of purposes we'll discuss later.

There are some big obstacles to all of us becoming aware of this. In our western society, one of the biggest is that many scientists deny even the existence of spirit. We hold scientists in high regard because of all the evident good they have done in so many fields. Not all scientists share that point of view, of course. Some of the most

2

respected quantum physicists have figured out that the world we perceive, which seems to be external to us and not under our control, is in fact not external and very much under our control.

But so many scientists believe that our consciousness is a result of matter reaching a certain degree of complexity, that anyone who maintains otherwise is considered by them to be ignorant of "established facts" in science. This makes such people and their ideas automatically not worthy of consideration or suitable for ridicule.

Since they are obviously so smart in their chosen fields of study, and since they collectively have done so much to make our lives easier, many of us accept their contention that if an idea or theory cannot be verified in scientific tests, then it cannot be accepted as "truth," or more simply, as the way things really are. Most of us haven't given it that much thought anyway, so we go along, and make them the official arbiters of what is to be considered acceptable when it comes to explaining what we are and how we got to where we are.

Unfortunately, they can't provide any solutions to the world's big problems or present a breakthrough that will address all the negative conditions that seem to surround us. But it is very, very important that we find those solutions, and that not just some of us find them. No, we *all* need to find them before we can move on to a dramatically better and more enjoyable existence for all of us. Ask yourself, could you be truly happy knowing that even a few of your fellow humans are existing in some miserable state, suffering either physically, mentally or emotionally?

Scientists are not the only obstacle. A lot of us are doing quite well in this physical world, so we don't like to think it's not the "real thing." The thought that we might not be able to enjoy the same physical pleasures in some afterlife existence, whatever it might be, is simply not appealing, so why waste time thinking about it.

On the other hand, a lot of us might not be doing all that well, which might predispose us to believing there is a better spirit world that we'll experience after this world. But we assume our minds are simply not developed enough to understand any of it, or why a Creator would create a world with so many problems, so we prefer not to think past the notion that no human can begin to comprehend the mind of God.

But dwarfing those obstacles is one basic problem. We are so preoccupied dealing with all the elements of our everyday lives, it is almost impossible for us to imagine that this physical world is not all there is, that it could all be an illusion of our own making, and that we will realize it's an illusion when we take leave of our physical body at death. It's tough to swallow.

Still, it is absolutely essential that we all come to those realizations if we are to experience a world that is many degrees of magnitude better than this one. So let's get started by addressing the contention that we are all spirits and the reasoning behind it.

4

Chapter 2 -- Logic Behind "We are all Spirits"— Input from Respected "Dead People"

Here's the reasoning behind the conclusion that we are all spirits. First, we seem to exist in a world where many people are suffering in many different ways, as noted in Chapter 1. Second, as much as we'd all like to believe in a loving, beneficent Creator who cares about us, we don't have any easily understood idea of why a Creator would create this instead of something better.

Yes, we can say that man, not God, is making this world as miserable as it is for many of us. But that leaves the question, if God is all-powerful and is aware of all things, and can see past and future, why create this mess when you know "ahead of time" it's going to wind up being a terrible mess?

There have been many scholarly cosmological and metaphysical explanations put forth over the centuries, but most of us won't take the time to understand them. We just don't relate to them. Besides, these explanations are by people living just as we are. What makes us think they should have all the answers the rest of us don't?

There must be something we're missing. There has to be something that explains in an easily understood way the inconsistency of what we experience on this planet and the assumption that there is a benevolent force behind its creation. If there are no such answers available, as many atheists assume, it makes sense that at the very least we should attempt to seek out every possible source for answers to such an important question. But if we can't find acceptable answers from all the very intelligent people who were alive when they addressed the problem, can we look anywhere else?

Well yes. We can ask whether any intelligence outside of our world has given us answers to these troubling questions that we can easily understand. One of the most logical places to start is with those of us who have lived on the planet like us, died so far as we can tell, and then came back to tell us what this existence is really all about. Makes sense, right?

Yes, but not everyone agrees. The immediate objection that arises is, "No one has ever come back to tell us what happens after we die, or why we're even in this less-than-ideal world to start with." That's a perfectly natural and valid reaction … until you start to search for evidence that perhaps many *have* come back to tell us. Many of the scientists we respect so much contend that's a fool's errand, since the only acceptable "Truth" is something we can verify in a lab.

If you accept their basic premise, you won't even start to look for evidence. They assume there can't be anything meaningful we'd find beyond the material world. But why not try? Even if we make fools of ourselves. After all, we have big problems and no answers.

Why not at least research a bit to see if these scientists could possibly be wrong? If we find nothing, it supports the assumption that they are correct. No harm in that. And if by chance we do find out some things, it opens the door to the possibility that we can indeed fix a lot of our problems.

I'm not a scholar and what little research I've done over the years has been done in my spare time when I haven't been working or spending time with my family, or on the hundreds of chores that fill a big part of most of our lives. So even though it took me 30 years to put together what I had learned in my first book, almost none of it is from firsthand experience. Rather I relied on what others experienced and documented in their books, assuming what they wrote was valid and really occurred. (I did know some of them and had a few firsthand experiences though.)

Relying so heavily on others wouldn't pass scientific muster of course. On the other hand, it seems logical that if a lot of people spent a lot of time with firsthand experiences, there is still room for someone, even a person with just ordinary intelligence, to do some synthesizing. Certainly there is room to look at the implications of what all these people experienced, what they discovered or learned from others, and then put some of those implications together and draw conclusions.

So what is offered here is not scientific or scholarly. You can decide for yourself whether something can be neither of those and still be "true," "significant," and helpful for a lot of people – especially those who struggle with a lot of difficulties and sometimes question why they are here and wonder how they can achieve more happiness and contentment while living their lives here.

In that "spirit," let's take a look at a summary of the evidence, reasoning and logic presented in more detail in my previous books.

Is there any evidence our personalities survive physical death?

There must be thousands of written accounts of people being contacted by dead relatives through mediums, also called psychics or channels, where the dead person presented a lot of "evidential," which is information that could only be known to the dead personality and the person receiving the information, thus "proving" they are the dead spirit they claim to be.

But in my opinion there is one example that stands out from all the rest as the best solid evidence by far that our personality survives our physical death. This is because of the quality and reputation of the medium, the number of respected, serious-minded personalities involved, the importance of the information they shared and the rigorous examination of their input by a panel of qualified experts, which included skeptics and a confirmed atheist. It was described in the book *The Airmen Who Would Not Die* by John G. Fuller.

Fuller described in detail the experience of a group of airmen in 1930 who served as officers and crew of R-101, a huge airship, on its maiden voyage to India. This ship was the pride of England, a "Titanic of the Air," and many of the leading officers of the Air Ministry were on board. Unfortunately it hit rough weather and crashed in France.

For several weeks afterward, many of the crew spoke through England's leading psychic, Eileen Garrett, whose reputation was beyond reproach. They shared many technical details about things that needed to change in the construction of the second craft already under construction, in order for it to be airworthy in a storm.

Their input was so detailed that it left no doubt in the minds of inquiry panels that these personalities had indeed survived physical death and were imparting important information in order to save the lives of any future crews and passengers. The situation was again investigated decades later by another panel of qualified individuals, one of whom was an atheist, and their unanimous conclusion was that personalities of these men had indeed survived physical death.

So yes, there is solid evidence that our personalities do survive death. There are as noted many other examples, but this event is the single most documented and it has never been refuted by any evidence or testimony to the contrary. But their purpose was not to tell us what death was like. Rather it was to save lives. Which leads to the next question.

Has any personality ever come back to tell us what death is like?

Yes. But you need to take into account how long they've been dead. And you need to discount the experience of anyone who had a "near-death-experience" (NDE) because they didn't really die. In *The Only Five Things You Need to Know* I summarized the evidence

9

from three people, all of whom died several decades ago, but from whom we have detailed accounts of their afterlife experiences.

Why these three? Well, when you start to look for this type of evidence, you are likely to come across much after-death communication that is relatively insignificant because it relates information meaningful to just a few people. Or perhaps it comes across as distorted, or not making much sense. That is due to the fact that people in spirit form after death are at many different levels of awareness and comprehension. Some are still in a sort of daze.

But you will also find information from personalities who were highly respected while they were alive, people of good character while living, who seemed to be well adjusted in their non-physical environment. They also had very good reasons for communicating with the living and did so with credibility. All of them provided "evidential" input, information that could be known only to the departed personality, in order to establish firmly that they were indeed who they claimed to be.

Frederic Myers

Frederic W. H. Myers died over a century ago in 1901. If you want to learn a great deal about him, you can read the 346-page book published by Hampton Roads in 2001, with an earlier publication in 1961 by University Press, *Human Personality and Its Survival of Bodily Death,* by F.W.H. Myers.

Myers was one of the founders of the British Society for Psychical Research. A highly educated man, he was a classical scholar best known for his essays on the Roman poets before he turned to psychic research. At the time of his death, he knew that one of the major obstacles to proving the survival of the personality was the possibility that the medium through whom messages came was telepathically tuning in to the contents of living human minds.

Myers solved this problem. After his death he gave bits and pieces of messages to mediums, as psychics and channelers were called then, in many different locations. The messages were received by automatic writing in trance, with Myers' signature at the end. The bits and pieces received by any one person didn't make any sense, and the mediums did not know one another. Neither were they familiar with the obscure classical sources which Myers, a leading classical scholar, liked to use. They were directed to send these meaningless messages to a central spot, where they were pieced together according to Myers' instructions.

When these meaningless messages were pieced together at the central spot, however, they made eminent good sense, and became known as the famous "cross-correspondences." Over a period of 30 years, there were 3000 of these messages, carefully investigated by the British Society for Psychical Research.

Myers was dead more than twenty years when he started communicating through Geraldine Cummins of Cork, Ireland. Over a period of seven years, from 1924 to

1931, he described the structure and conditions of life beyond death in detail. He described what he called "planes" of existence and discussed in detail seven major stages of development for the human spirit, corresponding to a growth in awareness of our consciousness. Just as awareness grows while we are in the body, so does it continue after death, he maintained.

His seven stages include the earth experience as the first, the condition immediately after death as #2, a very brief stage, he says, followed by entry into #3, a more stable world he calls "The Plane of Illusion," and then #4, a very beautiful experience, termed "The World of Eidos," or The Plane of Color. Qualified souls then progress to #5, "The Plane of Flame." He could not find words to describe #6 and #7, The Planes of Light and Timelessness, since he had journeyed only as far as #4, and knew of the others only through communication from other spiritual entities.

He was able to describe #4 in some detail from personal experience, and talked of entirely new and broader ranges of sound and color, a more intense and highly energized intellect, a more radiant and beautiful body, flowers in shapes unknown on earth, and more intense emotions, whether they be positive or negative.

The main work there, he says, is gaining greater awareness of how mind controls energy and life force. He described his ability to build up a likeness of himself and send it vast distances, controlling it from an enormous distance. What Myers says about the progress of a personality as it goes through these stages corresponds in many ways to what others have to say, though they do not necessarily describe seven distinct stages as he does.

Myers also expounded on many other subjects, including for example how bodies are sustained without food in the afterlife, and why over-attachment to earth possessions can be a problem that delays development of the soul's progress. He also described the contentedness of some souls to remain in the third plane for a long time, centuries sometimes, mistakenly thinking it to be the heaven of their earth beliefs and making no effort to progress further.

He explained, as others subsequently have, that our senses are precisely attuned to only a small slice of the wavelength spectrum, like a good radio receiver. Therefore we are not able to directly perceive other realities. But he points out that *it is not logical to conclude that the other realities do not exist because of the limitations of our senses,* any more than it would be logical to conclude there are no other broadcasting stations simply because we are tuned into just one. He spoke of cosmic and spiritual activity of great intensity around us all the time, of which we are not aware.

So what do you make of it? If you're a skeptic, you could probably find any number of explanations. But if you're not bent on reaching some preconceived conclusion, the most logical thing to conclude is that (1) Myers survived: (2) because proving the survival of our personalities after death was one of the most important things for him while he was alive, he chose a fairly convincing method to demonstrate it after he died.

Betty White

Betty died in 1939. Her husband, Stewart Edward White, was a well-known naturalist and world traveler, author of more than forty books in all, many of them about romance, adventure, and exploring new frontiers in pioneer settings. He held a Master's degree from the University of Michigan and was a graduate of Columbia Law School. He was totally uninterested in "matters of the occult" until Betty developed abilities as a medium, at first unwillingly in 1919, but later enthusiastically.

The quality of the information coming through Betty was of such high quality that Stewart White gradually gained high respect for it, regardless of its source. After accumulating over 400 typewritten pages in 18 months from the serious and scientific-minded entities speaking through Betty, who were called "The Invisibles" by the Whites, he summarized and published them in *The Betty Book,* published in 1937.

It was meant to be a description of the afterworld, to help guide those who die in their afterlife journey. The "Invisibles" generally confirmed what Frederic Myers and others had described regarding the levels of consciousness, but did not go into so much detail. White also published *The World Beyond* while Betty was alive.

In September 1939, six months after Betty died, she started speaking to her husband through the well-known medium Ruth "Joan" Finley, in Long Island. The Whites had known Ruth Finley when Betty was alive. Mrs. Finley was a respected journalist, and held positions that included Managing Editor of the *Washington Herald,*

Women's Editor of a newspaper syndicate, Associate Editor of *McClure's Magazine,* and a member of the steering committee of the National Federation of Business and Professional Women's Clubs. She was also the anonymous author of *Our Unseen Guest,* a widely read book on psychic phenomena in the 1920s, and was considered by many to be one of the most gifted trance mediums of the 20th century.

Speaking through Ruth Finley, for months Betty and her "Invisibles" gave scientifically oriented explanations of how the world we know is simply a part of a larger one. There was only one universe, she maintained. Time, space and frequency were three important concepts in the Invisibles' explanations of the universe, and those explanations were quite scientific and complicated.

Grossly oversimplified, the ideas they tried to get across were that time, space and motion, with which we're familiar, are each part of a larger concept. The essence of time is receptivity; of space, conductivity; and of motion, frequency. Matter is an "arrested frequency," Betty said. It is caught and slowed down, so to speak, in our space/time existence. There is no separation between our world and the world of the dead, she explained. One is merely an extension of the other.

She hadn't "gone anywhere," she explained, and made the same point emphasized by many others, that if we could change the focus of human frequency, we'd be able to see her instead of "looking through her" as we do. She repeated the idea posed by Frederic Myers, that a major difference between life and afterlife is the scope of

15

"awareness," with afterlife senses being able to tune into more realities.

"Lady Anne," one of the Invisibles, pointed out that consciousness is the only reality, and matter and mind are only aspects of it. Earth consciousness, she explained, is adapted to a universe in which there are many structures to bump into, not just physical but also mental, as when other people's ideas and thoughts obstruct you from doing what you want to do. Hence the term "unobstructed universe" to describe the larger universe where these obstructions do not apply.

Stewart White published these ideas in a book, *The Unobstructed Universe,* in 1940. It is a comprehensive and scientifically interesting account of life after death. It is also a compelling example of Betty speaking to her husband, getting across ideas she felt were important to spread.

She explained that they were all working hard on people who come over suddenly and don't know what is happening to them. It would help a lot, she said, if people had some understanding of the transitional phase, so they could make it more smoothly, and there would be less work for those on the other side who were helping them.

Given all of that, *The Unobstructed Universe* would be considered by most reasonable people to be a prime example of a highly respected person who has "died" giving us important information. It also conveys the warm emotional relationship that still existed between Betty and "Stewt," as she called her husband, after Betty died. In fact, he was so satisfied just by "feeling her presence" during the months since she had died, that he felt no need and had no desire for the verbal communication which started through Mrs. Finley in September. But, there was work to be done, and Betty was eager to get started.

The book is also significant for the many details Betty gives about the way she was operating, how she experienced the senses, traveled in time and space, perceived our universe, managed to communicate through "Joan," and influenced some events on earth in order to contact Stewt and get her message across. She talks about learning, rest, games, and other subjects familiar to us.

Time and again she emphasized the "hereness of immortality," the fact that there is only one universe, that she existed both in our world, and in the "unobstructed universe" that we do not experience. That's because her "awareness mechanism" could now take in a much larger field of experience in her afterdeath condition.

Betty also made it clear in simple terms that Consciousness creates form, not the other way around. It was the one and only reality, she said, and she explained how it manifested itself in different degrees in our universe, where the "true" realities of receptivity, conductivity and frequency were "suspended" or "arrested" in our time/space/motion world to create obstructions and matter. The consciousness frequency of each species exists *outside* our world, and manifests as that species when it is *inside* it, she maintained.

She also emphasized that Consciousness is always evolving. "There is, for example" she explained, "a

17

degree in the evolution of consciousness that we will call treeness; and in manifesting it becomes a tree. Now to that there is a corresponding frequency." The same thing goes for an electrical spark, she pointed out, and for all the different types of things that exist in our universe. Everything has consciousness, she said, but in different degrees.

A statement worth remembering … "Frequency is the eternal motion that never stops, and of which you are a part. It is your bit of quality: it's your I-Am. You are that frequency of consciousness that is a man; oxygen is that frequency of consciousness which is oxygen; a tree is that frequency of consciousness which is a tree."

There are also interesting discussions about the different types of "time." Sidereal time is what we know, but she makes us realize that "psychological time" of our own making is really more significant to our daily lives. True time, "orthic" time as she termed it, is different from those two, and she had a much greater ability to manipulate how she experienced it, than we have for manipulating how we experience sidereal time.

Another interesting concept, this one about space, is this: "Remove obstructions and you have "placeless space." Still another: "All you think and do is received and remains in time, though bodies and acts vanish from space." And another: "The Obstructed Universe (the one we live in) is for the purposes of birth and the individualization of consciousness."

In other words, in order to go through the experiences we do as humans, we've got to have the kind

18

of time and space we do, and "bump into things" with our low density bodies. And one more: "Your scientists have accepted the law of the indestructibility of matter; but I say to you that this law is only a corollary of the indestructibility of consciousness."

About the reality of heaven, purgatory and hell, Betty reinforces what others have said about their being of our own creation. All of us, she said, saint or sinner, have a tremendous fundamental urge to go on, to progress. But the person who has done all sorts of wrong on earth doesn't easily get adjusted and take control of manipulating his reality and progressing, as the urge would have him do. Consciousness is its own judge.

Peace and rest and ease do not come easily to those who have wronged seriously on earth. Instead of going forward quickly to a higher degree with its perceptions and pleasures, they linger in the lower degree. They suffer from frustrated urge. Some spend endless futile efforts trying to make restitution in the obstructed universe, further retarding themselves. Progress is made when the injured party arrives in the unobstructed universe: "That is a happier circumstance. That is where the 'seventy times seven' forgiveness thing comes true. They both understand: they both are free."

There are two more interesting points made by Betty. The first concerns the comparison of small events to great purposes. From Betty's viewpoint, she could see the general patterns or probabilities ahead for our obstructed universe, and was asked how this relates to free will.

19

Betty reinforced the existence of free will, and made a distinction between *intent* in time, and *an event* in time.

The intent is broad, and in the case of the largest intent, the evolution of consciousness, there is nothing we as individuals can do to stop it. Other large intents, such as the development of a democracy, can be influenced by us as individuals, but it is going to prevail regardless.

Events, on the other hand, are more malleable, and we can and do affect which events we will experience. An excellent analogy about how inevitable a given event might be, was likening it to a stream heading toward a waterfall. Just as the stream gains more acceleration and strength as it nears the edge of the waterfall, so events gain more solidity, more immunity against outside interference, as they approach culmination.

The second interesting and significant point is the comparison of the beauty of the universe Betty experienced, to the need and wisdom for us to stay focused on everyday living, and not to choose suicide. Joan, as Mrs. Finley the medium was called, was helped to briefly visit with her consciousness the world Betty was inhabiting. She described it.

She spoke of her sense of freedom and liberty, and the ability to go anywhere she might want. She also waxed enthusiastic about the beautiful bodies people there inhabit. She said they shone with light and color, and described Betty's body as a beautiful new color she had not seen anywhere else, made up of gold, a rich deep rose, and a sort of heavenly blue pulsating around her. It had a warm, sweet, very comforting feel to Joan. She could also hear what she likened to "the music of the spheres," postulated by Greek mathematicians. Beautiful voices sang all around her. She also understood that we can help those in that universe, just as they help us.

When presented with the problem that it was too attractive a world, so that it might discourage a lot of people from doing much at all but just wait for it, Betty replied in no uncertain terms. "The fact that you *are* a bit of individualized consciousness is itself a responsibility," she said. "Each bit has to grow sometime: it has to keep up with the evolutional law. *Consequently, the more quantity one attains in the obstructed universe, the more beautifully he will be able to go on in the unobstructed universe. Indeed, just that accumulation of quantity is the reason a long life is desirable.*"

Betty did not go easy on those who withdraw from life for "spiritual development" without adequate accomplishment in the ordinary things of life. She decried the tendency of some to become overzealous in their idealistic thinking and try to force it on others. She also had little patience with those who would piously devote themselves to "service" while leaving their own backyards cluttered.

She pointed out to "Stewt" that the mechanic who had come in that day to make household repairs "is gathering more quantity unto himself [experiencing personal soul growth] by going his own free-willed way according to his degree of quality, than if he had permitted you to force on him the reading of books he could not understand. ... There has been too much holierthan-thou stuff, and not enough recognition of the genuine adequacy of growth."

In that same session, Betty made a simple point that could well serve as a philosophy of life for many of us: "It is only the emotional things that really count. If people are big enough to live right emotionally, the concrete things can be overridden. Because - and I want you all to get this - because ***nothing that happens to an individual is as important as what that individual thinks about it.***"

And lest we get too proud of our achievements here on earth: "We do creative things here. There is not much original genius on your side; sometimes there is, but more often what you call genius is a dipping into what individuals here accomplish. Great artists have dexterity; and as a rule they are also great psychics. Sometimes they get our thought without being able to produce it, and that is a real tragedy.

"Scientists work on what you call scientific discovery, and are subject to sudden solutions to their problems. As in sleep." Betty commented on how the ideas of beings on her side are inserted into the minds of scientists (Thomas Edison?) during sleep, and made this interesting comment: "And do not think for one moment that high, low and in-between do not, at times, tap the infinity of our thought."

What do you make of all this? The simplest, most obvious explanation is that Betty White's personality survived and she saw an opportunity to do some good work after she died. She got in touch with her husband through a respected medium known to both of them, so that her husband could help her.

She provided plenty of "evidential" information, little details that could only be known to her and "Stewt," but "Lady Anne" made the following point about that, which is highly significant: "And if you have wanted a proof that I, that Betty, still exist, better than all the so-called evidential we could possibly give, that proof is in our building up the foundation of your own empirical knowledge into new and advancing thought."

Raymond Lodge (with some help from Frederic Myers)

Raymond Lodge was the son of Sir Oliver Lodge, who wrote about the communications from his son in the book *Raymond*. Oliver Lodge was one of England's most distinguished physicists, knighted for his work in atomic and electrical theory. Raymond was a British officer in France during World War I and was killed in action in September 1915. At that time, Sir Oliver was conducting extensive psychical research, working through three respected mediums, none of whom knew his true identity. Members of his family assisted him in the research.

The first message from Raymond came 11 days after he was killed. His mother was sitting with a medium who did not know her identity, and no questions were asked about Raymond. Still, Raymond came through with a message that Mrs. Lodge was to tell Sir Oliver that he had met some friends of his, specifically (Frederic) Myers.

Two days later, in an anonymous trance sitting with the same medium, he said he had a lot of friends helping him, and that he knew, as soon as he was better adjusted, he had a lot of work to do. Apparently he was confused at first and could not get his bearings, but "instructors and teachers," one of whom was Myers, helped him, and he was already beginning to feel brighter, lighter, and happier. A separate medium on the same day told Mrs. Lodge that Myers was helping her son to communicate.

In subsequent sessions Raymond confirmed Myers' guardianship and expressed deep gratitude to him. Raymond and Myers spoke together. Raymond got excited about his father's work in psychic research, exhorting him to push through barriers, so that more people could communicate with those who had passed on, and there would be fewer brokenhearted women on the earth side, and fewer dead soldiers to whom no one communicated on his side.

Myers explained that Raymond was traumatized initially, very disappointed, then recovered gradually. By the middle of November, two months after he died, he was feeling comfortable in his new environment and more sure of himself in his communications. What most reconciled him to his new environment was that things appeared so solid and substantial, including his grandfather and others who had met him, and the house his grandfather lived in, solid brick with trees and flowers. It got dark only when you wanted it to be dark. He hadn't yet found out whether thoughts alone formed all the buildings and flowers, or whether it was something more.

At that point, Raymond was preoccupied helping to orient soldiers who had been shot to death in the war, and could not yet see any indications of the future. He said at first he "wore" earth clothes, but gradually switched to the white robes popular there. His body, he said, was very similar to what he had before, but it didn't hurt as much when he pinched the flesh, and the internal organs did not seem constituted on the same lines. He had a new tooth in place of one that wasn't quite right, and knew a man who had lost an arm, but now had two.

When someone was blown to pieces, he explained, it took some time before the spirit body could reassemble itself completely. Interestingly, he said bodies should not be burned on purpose because they had some terrible troubles with people who were cremated too soon. He advised waiting seven days.

He observed that men and women seemed to have the same feelings toward each other, but with a different expression. There didn't seem to be any children born there. Some enjoyed eating what appeared to be earth food, and one fellow enjoyed a cigar. He explained that appetites for things like food, drink and cigars generally fade after people have been there for a while.

He could see the sun and stars, but didn't feel heat or cold, except when coming into contact with the earth plane. He gave several pieces of personal information known only to the family ("evidential") that established his identity. After a time, the urgency and content of his

25

information dwindles, as though he had his own affairs to pursue.

In response to a question from his father about a statement made by Myers, that the plane of existence Raymond was in was one of illusion, Raymond made interesting observations, with Myers' help. He said there were parallels between that plane and earth.

On both planes, he said, many things we need are created for us by the divine imagination, and many more things, like houses, clothes and jewels, are created out of our own imaginations. In both, they are created out of the available materials, and in both, the structures are temporary, meant to be used only until the person is ready to progress to the next higher plane. Earth objects are made of "matter," while objects in Raymond's sphere were made of much finer material, created by the power of mind.

Raymond said we live in a world of illusions, necessary for us to do our work, while he lives in an extension of that illusory world, the outer rim of it, so that he was more in touch with the "world of reality" than we are. Spirit and mind, from his perspective, are indestructible and belong to the world of reality, while other external things, necessary for a time, are really superfluous and temporary as far as the world of reality goes.

Raymond's observations are interesting and significant for the detail they provide, and for their consistency with the input of so many others, as he goes through the initial stages of existence after leaving the body.

Also significant is the advice of Sir Oliver Lodge for bereaved persons who inquire whether it would be advisable for them to devote the time and attention he did to communication with a departed loved one. Definitely not, was his advice. He was a student of the subject. For the average person, he recommended instead that they *"come to an understanding that their loved ones are still active and useful and interested and happy - more alive than ever in one sense - and to make up their minds to live a useful life until they rejoin them."*

Chapter 3 – Do "Living People" with Unusual Talents Agree?

Yes. People who had unusual talents while they were alive experienced and said things that would agree in principle with the input from the "dead people" mentioned in the previous chapter. "Dead people" is in quotes because, if they communicated with us after they departed the physical body, they aren't really "dead," are they? They're "living" in some other realm, the world of spirit. But let's take a look at three of the most impressive people who agreed (or agree) with them while they were living.

Edgar Cayce

Edgar Cayce (pronounced Casey) lived from 1877 to 1945, and dozens of books have been written about him. My favorite is *There Is a River* by Thomas Sugrue. Cayce discovered as a young boy that he had special abilities. As a young man he found he could go into trance and diagnose people's illnesses, regardless of where they were. He never charged any money for what he did, and so he was a bit frustrated when the unorthodox treatments he would prescribe for people while in trance would often be ignored by the person's doctor.

Although in trance Cayce could prescribe cures for the illnesses of thousands of people, he was totally unaware of what he had said when he woke up. But then in 1923 a wealthy fellow from Dayton OH, Arthur Lammers, visited and offered to finance the building of a hospital and medical school if Cayce would answer questions about religious philosophy on a regular basis.

Seeing a chance to help more people, Cayce agreed. Although the waking Cayce read the Bible continually, the answers he gave in trance supported the idea of reincarnation. When asked in trance how he came to develop his abilities, he explained he had been a doctor in Persia, and in another lifetime he was a soldier left to die on the battlefield in extreme pain for three days. During that time his consciousness separated from his body many times. He was a medium for some "bigger" aspect of himself, which included his doctor self, and as the wounded soldier he had developed his ability to go into trance easily.

Today in Virginia Beach VA, there are thousands of his readings available to study, at the Association for Research and Enlightenment. It is interesting to note that for many people he gave "life readings" in which he explained events in past lives and how they related to the present life. Many of them had lived in Atlantis, and Cayce described the breakup of Atlantis over three separate periods, the first about 15,600 B.C., when the mainland was divided into islands, and the last about 10,000 B.C., when the islands finally sank into the sea, apparently overnight. Cayce also made many predictions. Some did not materialize in this probable version of earth, but others proved out, most notably the shifting of tectonic plates, long before such shifts were even theorized by scientists.

One of the most significant things about Cayce was his ability to travel in space and time with his consciousness. In addition to traveling through the interior of the physical bodies of those he was giving a "reading" for in order to diagnose their illness, a number of times he visited what he called the Akashic Records. This is a "place" with a stored record of every event that has ever occurred in our universe, and also those in our future! Two of his readings demonstrate his abilities here dramatically.

One was for a young mentally challenged girl, where Cayce in trance explained that, years earlier, the girl had slipped getting out of a carriage and hit the base of her spine on one of the steps, which led to the mental condition. She recovered quickly when adjustments were made to her spine, following Cayce's instructions in trance.

A second instance occurred when a druggist in a different part of the country told the person Cayce had given the reading for, that he did not have the medicine Cayce had specified. Cayce in a subsequent trance session instructed the person to tell the druggist to look up on a high shelf, behind some other bottles, where the correct bottle was located, apparently placed there years earlier.

His experience confirms what "dead" people stated -- that our consciousness is not limited to our body, that time and space are just illusions we work with to achieve growth during our earth incarnations, and that we are indeed much more than we think we are. Cayce often maintained that he did not have special powers, and anyone could eventually learn to do what he did, with enough effort.

His readings and the evidence which indicates they were consistently on target, are on file today in Virginia Beach VA, where the Association for Research and Enlightenment continues a variety of activities based on ideas contained in Cayce's readings. They constitute one of the largest and most impressive records of psychic perception ever to emanate from a single individual. There is an entire library in which you can research his readings, relevant records, correspondence and reports, cross-indexed under thousands of subject headings, and placed at the disposal of psychologists, students, writers and investigators.

Now you can take the position that just because Cayce's medical diagnoses and prescriptions proved effective, that doesn't mean his explanations about our having many lives with connections among them, are correct. On the other hand, it seems logical to assume that, since the source of his medical knowledge was correct and helped a lot of people, that same source would probably speak intelligently about other things, and should therefore be listened to with respect.

This is a source, remember, that not only makes a diagnosis, but also directs a druggist many miles away to look behind some old bottles on a dusty shelf to find a medicine the druggist didn't even know existed. Rather than dismiss the explanations of life which an intelligence like that has to offer, wouldn't it be better to attach a lot of credibility to the information it imparts, unless and until proven otherwise?

But now to the reason why we're talking about Edgar Cayce in this book. It is this. When questioned in trance by Lammers as to how he first entered the earth plane, Cayce explained that he was part of a group of *spirits* traveling through the universe, when they were attracted to earth and the idea of joining their consciousness with the physical animal body consciousness of humans on that planet.

At first they were well aware of their true nature as spirits when they were in bodies, but gradually over time and incarnations they lost that awareness and thought they were only the human consciousness inside a body. Then gradually they became more aware of their true nature and, each at its own pace, started to realize to varying degrees that they were actually spirits, temporarily ensconced in a physical body each time they incarnated. The key point there is that they were a group of *spirits* traveling through the universe when they decided to try out earth life!

As noted in *We Are All Tourists,* they were travelers, tourists if you will, deciding to experience a version of this life that we know. Sugrue's book does not go into it in depth, but presumably this would be one stop on their journey, and there would be many others.

The reincarnational phase of going into and out of physical bodies, experiencing firsthand time, space, individualized consciousness and all the other root

32

assumptions that prevail here, is something these spirits wanted to do, much as a tourist might want to visit museums, climb pyramids or experience wild river rapids in a rubber raft, but then move on after the experience is realized for whatever excitement and learning it brings.

Toward the end of *There Is A River* Sugrue summarizes in 15 pages Cayce's comments on philosophy and the journey of souls. Everyone who channels has a "filter" affected by his or her own beliefs, and since Cayce was an intensely religious Christian, some of the material has a heavy traditional religious flavor, but much of it is simply stated as "the way things are" once you are not limited in awareness by being in a physical earth body. It gives some philosophical background as to why we are all spirits.

It talks about a "sea of spirit," content and aware of itself, that desired to express itself and have companionship. *All of creation is an expression of its thought.* The separate "mind" it created did everything it imagined. The material terms this sea of spirit "God." **The souls, that which we are,** fit into all this by experiencing all of creation, unlimited with free will and the knowledge that it is an individualized consciousness but also a part of God. **So "God" would know itself through the experiences of these souls, which were powerful, eternal creators of whatever they wished.**

As noted earlier, for those souls attracted to experience within the earth bodies, at first they only lightly inhabited the bodies, remembering their true identity as souls, but gradually descended into

33

"earthiness," remembering their true selves only in dreams, stories and fables. *As a result of their yearning for lost memories, parts of these souls gradually developed religion, philosophy and science in an attempt to explain what they felt, but no longer knew, to be true.* As you'll see in a later chapter, it is notable that science was included as one of the fields the souls developed to explain what they felt to be true.

In this explanation, our present era is described as one of great spiritual darkness, the kind of darkness that comes just before the dawn. (It is also probably why the best evidence for us being spirits, not just physical matter, occurred not recently but rather, from 100 to 30 years ago.) It also contends as noted that science, philosophy and theology are approaching a point of merger.

In this explanation, Christ is positioned as a soul that had completed its experience of creation and had returned to God, becoming a companion and co-creator, interested in the plight of its brother souls "trapped" in earth. So it took form itself from time to time to act as teacher and leader to help lead man back to his true nature.

The entity had to be male in order to be active in the civilizations where it entered. As Enoch and Melchizedek it was not born and did not die, but instead just took on flesh. In later incarnations it set a pattern for man by being born of woman. He came in as Joseph, Joshua, Jeshua and Jesus.

The summary in Sugrue's book and Cayce's life experience combine to form a strong body of information

34

that closely correlates with the input of dead people when it comes to who and what we are, and why we are here.

Bob Monroe

Bob Monroe died in March 1995. While he was living, he was the best known and most credible out-of-body traveler in the Western Hemisphere. He had a long and successful career in broadcasting, had a background in engineering, and was a pilot, so he was in many ways a down-to-earth American businessman. I knew him slightly, but had friends who knew him well.

In 1971 he wrote his first book, *Journeys Out of the Body,* which chronicles his experiences when, at first involuntarily, his consciousness began to leave his body. Once he got over his fear, he was able to leave his body at will. At first he'd just travel down the street or around town and gather convincing evidence he had indeed been where he said he'd been. Then he traveled to more exotic places, one of them a universe where he joined his consciousness with another version of himself, getting that version of himself in trouble once or twice.

Around that time he set up what is now called *The Monroe Institute,* where he worked with others on sound frequencies and patterns, eventually developing *Hemi-Sync,* a method for using sound waves to enable people to quickly go into the *theta* state of brainwave patterns, one of deep concentration, previously achieved for the most part only after a long period of meditation. In that state, the brain can follow frequencies that are introduced, and so they introduced "sound recipes" associated with

35

memory, creativity, concentration, etc.

For our purposes the significant things about Bob Monroe are his descriptions of his travels over the years in two subsequent books, *Far Journeys* and *Final Journey,* and the fact that the institute he set up has enabled many people to go into *theta,* and then for a number of them, to travel out of body as he did, visiting various times and "places" in this and other universes.

In his books, Bob explained that he was able to make contact with a variety of intelligent personalities who were capable of assuming various forms to help teach him about illusions and other matters, **and who at times assumed no form at all.**

Bob was an excellent observer, knew the best questions to ask, and recorded the answers accurately. He was able to travel through "rings" of existences beyond earth, where different types of personalities dominated. They ranged from those spirits who didn't yet realize they were dead, through those at various levels of awareness and training, all the way to those preparing for their last sojourn on earth.

His input tracks closely with what Frederic Myers, Betty White and others said. That includes what he called the *Belief System Territories,* where you can create whatever you want just by thinking about it, and where many stay for a long time, thinking it is the heaven of their earth beliefs, until a guide "taps them on the shoulder," so to speak, informing them they have a lot of training and growth left, so they might as well get started.

He also visited one probable version of earth around

the year 3000, where his guides emphasized this was only one of many probabilities. In that probable future there were no factories, roads, planes, cars, houses, phones or any other indicators of "modern existence."

Spirits who chose to come to earth at that time understood they were basically spirits, and went in and out of different bodies as they pleased. Physical bodies were constructed from earth materials, preserved and protected in special "energy cocoons," and available for inhabiting when a spirit feels it could learn something from the experience. They did not have to eat to sustain themselves. Instead they just stretched their arms out to absorb life-sustaining energy from the universe.

By that time, many spirits currently in a physical body do not bother to come back to earth. Those who do primarily want to join their consciousness with other species to get their perspectives. Bob tried it out and joined with, among other things, an eagle, a fish, a leaf, a storm cloud and a panther.

The information Monroe received also explained how a particular consciousness might become attracted to living through a series of earth lives. In his third book he gave an overview of why we as spirits would even bother to experience earth lives. Essentially, it has to do with the emotional experiences you can get while here, gifts that we ultimately bring back to our Creator, which knows itself partly through these experiences.

A "larger self," of which each of us is a part, apparently cannot return to the Creator until every earth personality that is part of it has learned its lessons, experienced all it needs to experience, and freed itself from desires associated with the earth form of life. This is an uplifting and hopeful idea to keep in mind. It means everyone eventually gets forgiven, no matter how atrociously they have behaved on earth, and is united with the Creator. No one gets left behind or is assigned for eternity to some horrible fate.

Another beautiful concept Monroe actually experienced is that the energy we send out as a result of our emotional experiences is amplified many times and returned to us as loving energy that sustains us still more. So we can think of ourselves as power sources who generate more loving energy than we take in, spew it out wherever it's needed, and then this energy is amplified even further by the bigger spirit of which we are a part.

As a result of his direct experiences Bob Monroe came to believe that you can live more than one life simultaneously, that probabilities exist, that the "space-time illusion" in which we exist is a camouflage reality, and that there are a great number of other realities for us to explore when we're out of body for a short period while we're alive, or a longer period when we die.

What Monroe has to say is particularly significant because:

❑ He spoke from direct experience.

❑ Despite many opportunities, he never attempted to sensationalize or exploit his astounding experiences in order to gain high public visibility or reap huge financial returns.

❏ He helped many individuals from all walks of life to achieve out-of-body experiences and make contact with other intelligences on their own.

❏ As a businessman, family man, and a likable human being, he was someone the average person could easily relate to. He was a living example of how we can combine everyday living with the development and use of abilities that many, if not all of us, possess.

❏ He was cooperative with established psychiatrists and psychologists, and developed close personal and professional relationships with many of them, as he sought to examine and evaluate the nature and significance of his experiences. He was driven in part by the hope that their participation and study would ultimately bring about a situation where the things he experienced and learned could bring about tangible benefits for a broad cross-section of society.

Joe McMoneagle

Joe is married to Bob Monroe's daughter, Nancy. He was the lead psychic in the Army's 20-year program dedicated to using psychic powers to help the United States in matters of vital national security. He has been in the Oval Office more than once, and in private life has been a "remote viewer" for many years, often retained by large corporations. He has authored *The Ultimate Time Machine* and a number of other books.

If Joe is given any two of three reference points, he can go to the destination desired. The three points are the time, the longitude/latitude, and an event. He has demonstrated this a number of times in controlled experiments and for television audiences around the globe. In one instance, unbeknownst to him, he was given coordinates for the planet Mars, and when he traveled there, he noted that very big people must live there, guessing that he must have been somewhere in South America.

Like Bob Monroe, Joe believes in probabilities, and he too traveled to the year 3000, visiting what was apparently a different probability from what Bob Monroe experienced. In the preface to one of his books he quotes from the entity Seth discussed in the next chapter, channeled by Jane Roberts in Elmira NY. In response to my direct questions, both Joe and Bob Monroe agreed that Seth had it pretty much right in his description of the various spiritual and physical realities, including the one we experience on a daily basis.

Chapter 4 – The "Deadest of the Dead"—
The Entity Seth

Edgar Cayce and Bob Monroe, while they were living in a human body, both had experiences and got information that indicates they were traveling through the universe, much as tourists might, came upon the earth Time-Space Illusion, and decided to try it out, resulting in a number of lifetimes as humans on earth. Now we will take a look at a spirit entity who explains that, just like Cayce and Monroe, we are all spirits and the earth experience is just one of many we have in a timeless universe, some in pure spirit and some with a material form.

My earlier books contain a lot of input from the Seth entity, especially from two books authored by Jane Roberts, who channeled Seth. They are *Seth Speaks* and *The Nature of Personal Reality,* the 2nd and 4th of the twenty or so books Jane and her husband Rob produced, all published originally in the 1970s and 1980s by Prentice-Hall, a highly respected publisher at the time.

It is important to note that in the Introduction to some of her books Jane shares her thoughts in depth as to the precise nature of Seth and "his" relationship to her subconscious and her soul. She thoughtfully considered many alternative explanations before accepting the "reality" of Seth as an entity separate from her but closely related to her on a soul level. Her initial skepticism and insightful analysis while delving into these questions give the information imparted by Seth a good deal of credibility in my opinion. The total body of material he shared gives it even more credibility from my perspective. I highly recommend that you read both of the books mentioned above.

I believe Seth gave us the most complete and accurate description of the true nature of the reality we perceive, and how it is created and supported by deeper underlying realities. He said he had completed all his lives on earth, and was now part of a group of spirits who slip in and out of different realities such as ours, to inform the inhabitants there of the true nature of the reality they are experiencing. Spirits at his level of development have three main choices, to be a teacher, creator or healer, and he is part of a teaching group.

So he does not speak from the perspective of someone who has just died, or who is between physical lives. Rather it is from the perspective of a spirit who has completed all "his" earth lives (he incarnated many times as a female) and has access to a much greater body of knowledge and experience, not just his own, but also that of a number of other spiritual entities.

Probable Selves and Free Will

Seth stated that we are all just one probable version of ourselves, and that for every major decision in life to which we gave a lot of thought, there is another version of us that thinks he or she is the official you or me. Taken all together, the various probable versions of ourselves constitute the total us, at least at the focus personality level.

Because of probabilities and our free will, Seth stayed away from predictions, because the you or me who exists right now might experience any of a large number of probabilities in the future. His only prediction over 20 years of dictating many books was that by the year 2075 many of us will understand that we are essentially eternal, powerful spirits, whereas the physical universe we perceive is a temporary illusion.

Consciousness Expands Beyond the Body & We Play Many Roles

We will all know our consciousness is not restricted to our physical bodies. We'll understand that, as human focus personalities, we are playing a role, one of many we play, and that others, no matter how low or exalted their position, are doing the same, so we won't look down on others. We might, for example, be a successful businesswoman in one life and a ragged homeless man begging in the streets in another life.

We'll be aware of many of our "past" existences, and if we play the role of victim in one, for example, we might (or might not) at the same time choose to be playing the role of killer in another. We'll also be much more aware of what goes on "in between" lives.

We Co-Create Our Experience & There is no Death

We will understand that we have a much closer connection than we realize to the physical objects and environments we are co-creating. We'll be able to "travel" in time. We'll understand there is no "death" as we think of it, just an expansion of our consciousness when it is no longer restricted by being in the physical body.

We Are All Very Powerful & More Than We Think We Are

Seth contends that we are each much more, and much more powerful, than we give ourselves credit for. Not only are we more than what we think ourselves to be in one physical lifetime, which I refer to as our focus personality, but our larger identity, the full extent of our being, is much more than the combination of *all* our reincarnational personalities.

As we normally think of ourselves, we assume we are conscious beings in a physical body, generally not able to extend our consciousness beyond our physical bodies. The self we're aware of is our ego self, the part of us that deals with the external world as we perceive it. But another part of us, our "inner self," is aware not only of our physical world, but also many other realities, some physical and some not.

Our inner self is also the part of us that connects us to what I call our Big Self, which is a larger "gestalt" or structure of consciousness, that is the source of energy not only for us, but also for many other focus personalities. It projects a portion of itself into various realities, not just the one we know, and that includes not only our past and present selves, but the past and present selves of other

44

focus personalities, and the "probable" versions of all of us.

Probable versions of ourselves are spun off continually whenever we give a lot of thought and emotion to a decision and decide to make one probable action the one we experience in the physical world. So someone might give a lot of thought to becoming a pilot, for example, but also to becoming a professional swim instructor. After a lot of consideration, they decide on becoming a pilot, and they become one. In another probability, however, there is a version of them that became a professional swim instructor. Both versions are real in their respective realities, and both think they are the "authentic" self, totally unaware of the other probable version of themselves.

With all the major decisions millions of us make in the course of our lives, and all the major decisions made by localities, states and countries, corporations, non-profits, social agencies, associations, clubs and much more, you can see that the world of probabilities must be vast indeed. It follows that our Big Self, just to be aware of all these realities in all these time frames, and to provide the energy for all the individual personalities who create them, must be an impressive and powerful entity indeed. **Well, that's who you are!**

The Ego Portion of Us Deals with HTSI

For purposes of dealing with different realities, we assign portions of ourselves specific duties, such as dealing with our Human Time-Space Illusion (HTSI) as a focus personality, but there is in fact no real division. We are our Big Self, our soul if you like, currently inhabiting a physical body while other portions of ourselves (of our Big Self) are focused elsewhere in many different realities, helping to co-create them as we co-create this one. We are indeed powerful, eternal *and multi-dimensional* beings.

We Can Scarcely Imagine the Majesty of Ourselves

Seth explains that the soul, that's us, is a multidimensional, infinite act, with each minute probability brought into existence somewhere, materialized in a physical reality or actualized in a non-physical one. But while we are focused so tightly in a three dimensional reality as we are now, we're not able to understand or experience the majesty of our own greater existence.

He mentions more than once that our slightest thought or emotion gives birth to worlds. Not only that, but it is impossible for any idea to die or any ability to go unfulfilled. Each probable system creates other systems, and all systems of reality are "open" so that any one of them can affect the other. Any act brings forth an infinite number of unrealized acts that will find materialization or actualization somewhere.

We are all in the center of a gigantic "cosmic web" of probabilities, so that thoughts and emotions go forth from each of us in all physical directions and in non-physical directions invisible to us, while we are also the receiver of signals, thoughts and emotions coming from others. The energy exchange that we set in motion appears to us as objects and events, but it also appears to personalities in other realities, in forms or non-forms suitable for the root assumptions in their reality, which might or might not closely resemble ours.

We Are More than our Consciousness

Difficult as it might be to imagine existence without consciousness, we are not just our consciousness. It is an essential characteristic of ours, something that belongs to us at both the Big Self "soul" level and the level of us focus personalities, but the soul (which is who we really are) is more than just its consciousness. It is a focal point of reality from which other realties spring forth, and its creations roam far and wide, so to speak.

There Are No Limits to Us

Here are some of the most important things to remember about your soul. It is not something we have. It is what we are. It must by its nature be forever changing and it has its existence not just in our little reality, but in many other dimensions. Its fulfillment does not depend on arriving at any point, spiritual or otherwise. There are no limits to it. Boundaries would enclose it and deny it freedom, so it cannot have boundaries.

Seth claims it is **the most highly motivated, most highly energized, and most potent consciousness-unit known in any universe.** As such, it contains unlimited potential, and within it are personality potentials that are beyond our present comprehension. *This is us, our own* *souls, that he is talking about.* Each of us is our soul focused in the Human Time-Space Illusion. Defined that way, each of us is a "prime identity," one that is a gestalt or combination of many other individual consciousnesses.

It is (we are) an unlimited self that can and does express itself in many ways, forms and non-forms, while still retaining its own identity. It can merge with and travel through other energy fields to explore literally endless possibilities of development and expansion, but all the while retains its own "I-am-ness," as Seth terms it.

The positive realizations to take away from all this are that our soul possesses the wisdom, information and knowledge that is part of the experience of all its personalities, and because there is continuing inner communication among its personalities and no closed systems of reality, the knowledge of one is available to any other, right now, in our present moment. It is only our limited perception, necessary to this point for us to deal effectively with conditions in HTSI, that prevents us from realizing that. **But we are a soul right now.**

The soul within us is perceiving right now, but its methods of perception are much broader, as they were before our birth and after our so-called "death." It doesn't suddenly change its methods of perception when we are born or die. It's only the focus personality portion that does that, and our focus personalities, you and me, will never be destroyed or lost. It will continue to grow and develop and expand what the soul knows itself to be. We focus personalities remain distinct and individual, but we will also know that we are one manifestation of our soul.

Making Sense of Earth Life – the Time-Space Illusion

If all that is so, the question arises, how do we make sense of this earth life we're living? In previous books I've noted that when the soul enters the human body in an incarnation, it is somewhat similar to putting on 3D glasses or a virtual reality headset, so that we experience things differently from the way we would when we are in pure spirit form. We do this in order to play the "earth game."

We All Agree to the "Root Assumptions" of our Reality

We temporarily stamp out our awareness of our own greater existence, so we can experience the emotions that us humans are so capable of. In order for the game to be played, all of us who incarnate need to agree on certain basic root assumptions of our reality here, with those assumptions serving as the framework in which our little reality drama can be played out.

And so we all agree that time is real, a series of moments, that an objective world exists out there separate from us, independent from our creation and perception of it, that we are separate from each other with each of us locked within physical bodies, limited in terms of what we can do and make not only by time but also by space. We all agree, as our scientists do, that all perception comes through the physical senses, from outside of us, and that no information can come from within, from any "inner senses."

We agree to have good and evil, and that one of our

49

principal operating mechanisms will be cause and effect, as opposed to bringing an object or event into existence just by focusing on it with intensity, so that it materializes or "manifests."

Operating by these root assumptions in this particular stop in our tour through many universes, we are temporarily forced to focus tightly on the actions within our play. From our soul's larger perspective, the lives we lead in the various reincarnations are our participation in several plays, with all of them existing at one time. (Some who are resting or otherwise occupied between lives will try to communicate to those active in the play how things really are, but in between lives they are still "in the wings" so to speak, not yet fully aware of the total larger reality in which we all exist.)

Why Do We Play the Game?

We do all this so that, among other purposes, we can experience emotions we couldn't otherwise experience – things like joyful surprise, the dawning of a new romance, the agony of betrayal and seeming defeat, the anticipation of something good happening to us, the excitement of not knowing how a sporting event, or a battle, might turn out. And we're the richer for it. The emotions are permanently a part of our soul experience, and so we possess a certain "earthiness" that is not possessed by those consciousnesses who choose not to participate in our grand illusion.

But in the process we are also learning how to be co-creators. We are learning to handle the responsibility that

50

belongs to any individualized consciousness that has been given the power to create. Here in "earth school" we learn how to create responsibly, so that when we go on to bigger and better things, we'll create realities that are more joyful and fulfilling than what we're creating right now.

Meanwhile, the rocks and stones and mountains and the earth itself are all living camouflage realities, temporary illusions we co-create while they are necessary for our learning to proceed. That's not to say that physical reality is false. It is just a physical picture we create that is one of the infinite number of ways of perceiving the many guises through which consciousness expresses itself.

Physical reality is an illusion, yes, but a "real" illusion that is caused by a greater reality, and the illusion has purpose and meaning. The reality we perceive is an interpretation of larger events as they intrude upon our three-dimensional reality. The events themselves are mental, not physical. So what we perceive through our senses, while it has little resemblance to the facts of the greater underlying reality that supports it, is useful, helpful and real.

We're Learning

We are learning in a three-dimensional context how our emotional and psychic existence can create all sorts of physical forms and events. This enables valuable training, Seth points out, where we eventually learn that our physical environments are not objective things that exist independently of us, that they are indeed extensions of ourselves, materialized mental acts that extend outward from our consciousness.

In that regard, Seth says he is a "personality with a message." The message is that we create the world we know and we've been given the most awesome gift of all, the ability to project our thoughts and emotions outward into physical form. But with it comes responsibility. We create both the glories and the terrors we experience. Until we realize that, we will refuse to accept the responsibility.

Apparently some of us err on the side of caution, afraid of projecting our ideas and desires outward, because we have an underlying belief that what is powerful is evil. That is certainly understandable enough, given the well supported observation over the centuries that "power corrupts," and absolute power corrupts absolutely. We have only to read the international news stories of many countries ruled by dictators today where this is obviously the case.

But Seth insists that the universe is a good universe, one that knows its own vitality, and that vitality is within each one of us. We needn't hesitate to encourage it freely, he maintains, because our own nature is a good nature and we can trust it.

Our Major Obstacle

The major obstacle for us in trying to make sense of HTSI is our belief system. If we believe only in the context of this one life, born only to death and annihilation, then we will not use our freedoms in this existence. If we believe we are stuck in time and in our bodies, at the mercy of events that seem to happen to us, before which we are often seemingly powerless, then we will not get past the physical limits imposed by our limiting beliefs. We will not come to realize that our thoughts, alone and intertwined with others, form reality.

On the other hand, when we do achieve that realization, we are no longer a slave to events. Seth maintains that to get out of the box we've created for ourselves, we simply have to learn the methods, and they've been known for centuries. Basically they come down to listening – listening to our inner self – which theoretically we can do anytime we decide to put our minds to it.

Another obstacle to making sense of earth life is that we are necessarily so tightly focused on it that we emphasize all the similarities that bind us together, and ignore the differences. So there might be perfect agreement among a group of us that the couch we are sitting on is solid, and that there is empty space between those of us sitting on it, and between our couch and someone else's swivel chair.

If we were to focus instead on the dissimilarities, apparently we'd be amazed that we can form any notion at all of an organized, structured reality. We'd see that the space between people is not vacant, that it is full of molecules and electromagnetic field forces, that the "couch" we are sitting on is not solid, and that we are sitting on emptiness that we do not perceive with our tight focus. Through our physical senses we impose an organization on what we perceive, and thereby create it.

Each of us Constructs our own Unique Idea of Reality

In fact, none of us perceive the same couch as the next person. We perceive only "idea constructions" and cannot see the idea constructions perceived by someone else. Telepathically though we all agree that the couch is there, and that it is in a particular "place" in space.

Likewise, when a pretty girl enters a crowded room, no two people "see" the same girl. Each of them constructs their own idea of the person they perceive. Each perceives their own creation. So there is not just one of her. There are as many of her as there are people in the room.

In the same manner, each of us transposes our individual ideas on all the atoms and molecules we perceive. Physical matter is not solid unless we believe that it is. The organization we perceive is transposed from within us -- to seemingly outside of us. That is the process by which each of us forms the reality that we know, and telepathically we combine with others to create the reality that we consider common to all of us. At our soul level we know this, but at our conscious focus personality level we pretend not to know.

The objects we perceive are themselves symbols – symbols that stand for inner experience. There are mass physical symbols that we all agree on, such as mountains and seas, as well as private personal symbols, such as our bodies and immediate environment. In fact, the whole structure of physical life as we know it is a symbolic statement made by groups of entities who choose to work with physical symbolism – that's us, or at least those of us who choose to stop on our tour and experience the Human Time-Space Illusion.

Our Body is a Symbol

Our body is a symbol for what we are, or what we think we are, and those might be two very different things. Ailments, strengths, good times, bad times, our entire life in fact, is a statement in physical terms, standing for inner experience. That statement is written upon time (as we understand it) … as the medium on which we write. From that perspective, illness and suffering are the results of misdirection of creative energy. Here Seth gave us my favorite line, **"Suffering is not good for the soul unless it teaches you how to stop suffering."** In learning how to handle our creative energy, he explains, we often misdirect it, ***thereby automatically bringing us back to important inner questions we need to solve.***

Think of our World as our Own Painting

It might or might not be helpful for you, but Seth uses an analogy here of a painting depicting a great battle. Mankind errs, brings ill health, death and desolation upon himself, but he is still using his creative abilities to create a world. By observing his creations, he learns to use his abilities better. The work is still a creative achievement, though it might portray tragedy or unspeakable terror, just as the painting portrays intense suffering and death.

Likewise, in wars we use creativity to create destruction. Illness and suffering, he points out, are a by-product of the learning process, created by us, but in themselves quite neutral.

Our symbols are a way of expressing feelings that can't be expressed adequately through words. They will appear differently in the various stages of consciousness. He gave an interesting example, the emotion of joy, which he claims changes the objects in the perceiver's environment, so that the perceiver sees them in a far brighter light, with more clarity and far more vividly. Then the environment gives him feedback that reinforces his joy. This has been the subject of many songs, but it was especially beautifully expressed in Andrew Lloyd Webber's musical *Aspects of Love* in the song *Love Changes Everything,* which you can listen to on YouTube.

The Impact of Fears

Just as we need to be continually changing and developing, so do our symbols, which need to be fluid and ever-changing. If instead they are used as a sort of container to house original experience that defies change, they end up deceiving rather than illuminating. When that happens, fear is always involved. Fears act as a distorting lens and a barrier to free flow. This builds up pressure, and symbols of an explosive nature then act as releasing agents, methods to reduce the pressure. As Seth put it, **without physical storms we would all go insane.** Given the immense pressure on millions of people around the globe right now, we can expect a lot of very powerful storms.

How do we Reconcile a Good God with Evil?

One of the toughest things for us to deal with in earth life is the presence of evil. Seth explains that opposites have validity only in our system of reality, and that good and evil are opposites, just as up is the opposite of down. (He showed his sense of humor when he pointed out that Christ could just as well have disappeared sideways.) Good and evil effects, just like up and down, are basically illusions, as all opposites are. Instead, in the larger reality all acts are part of a greater good.

We focus personalities do not perceive wholes, but just portions. The evil we perceive is … a distorted version … of a tiny portion … of much larger events … that are intruding on our three-dimensional universe.

By stretching the bounds of your intellect, you can almost understand that and accept it, but it is almost impossible to accept emotionally and difficult to internalize intellectually when the news we see each day is of mass killings, girls sold into sex slavery and innocent people burned to death by terrorists. But we need to try if we are ever to get past this world we're currently experiencing.

Why "Evil Effects" are Necessary

In my opinion, the explanation for evil easiest to comprehend was given in Seth's *Nature of Personal*

Reality. It has to do with the experiment in consciousness that is ours and how it started. Previously we had the same kind of consciousness as the animals, where we knew we were connected with and part of nature. Animals know unconsciously they are unique and have a place in the scheme of being. They have an innate knowing that they survive physical death. They have no need to justify their existence, no conscience or sense of guilt. They have a built-in "state of grace" and their behavior follows their instincts.

The experiment with human consciousness we are living in was to take on the ability to reflect, so we could think back on our past and project into our future. This is an interesting and complex experiment indeed, witness the human condition as we currently perceive it. A key point is that, by its nature, this experiment requires free will. As self-conscious beings we regulate our reality by our beliefs. As Seth put it, we have "the responsibility and the gift, the joy and necessity" of working with our beliefs and choosing the personal reality we desire.

In this experiment we have freedom to choose any belief we want, including one that says we are unworthy, with no right to our existence, and we must be "saved." **In order for our consciousness to develop in our experiment, we had to have the freedom to explore all ideas individually and as a group.** So we must have free will. That includes ideas that, when materialized, appear in no uncertain terms to be evil, and so we meet with effects that appear to be evil. Despite these effects, Seth maintains that in basic terms there is no evil, and as we

58

develop as a human race we will eventually understand that all seeming opposites, such as good and evil, are "other faces of the one supreme drive toward creativity."

Again, when we are face-to-face with any of these evil effects, it is almost possible not to conclude that evil exists. It requires a trust and a realization that what we perceive is not reality, but rather our idea of reality as we construct it. That is very difficult. It is especially difficult when we think the world is material only, and there is no spiritual reality supporting it.

The Devil

While we are on the subject of evil, it is only natural to think of "the devil." The devil, in Seth's terms, is a "superlative hallucination." The devil idea is a mass projection of certain fears. The older religions apparently understood that, and understood that storms are highly creative natural events. Here we need to remember the point made in my earlier book about Christ's crucifixion - that thoughts are real, that the mass thoughts projected over the centuries about the crucifixion have their own reality, and can have a far greater impact on our physical lives than the events that were actually physical at that time.

Likewise, the mass thoughts projected over the centuries about the devil concept have their own reality, and can impact us in our physical reality even though no such devil exists outside of those thoughts and hallucinations. Just ask the poor women who were burned for being "witches" in Salem, Massachusetts.

There are No "Secret Thoughts"

There is one more characteristic of HTSI that deserves mention. It is the assumption that our thoughts are secret from one another. At the level of daily conscious living they seem to be, but it is apparent through telepathic communication that they are not. In that regard, the experiences of Joe McMoneagle, who as noted earlier can travel with his consciousness to any time and place, are instructive.

He was the chief psychic in an army program that lasted 20 years. A government agency wanted to test him by having him travel to their labs and observe what one of their chief scientists was doing for one day. They were not surprised when he was able to tell them what the scientist did, but they were understandably concerned when Joe was able to tell them what the scientist was thinking while he performed certain chores.

What are the Implications if All This is Correct?

At this point you can either accept all that has been stated so far, accept just some of it, or deny that any of it could be an accurate description of reality. If you take that last option you'd be in good company. In August 2017 I read a book review in The Wall Street Journal by Joanna Bourke. Ms. Bourke is a professor of History at Birkbeck, University of London, and is the author of a book titled *What It Means to be Human.* So she's quite learned, with a highly respected position in academia.

Likewise, the author of the book she reviewed, *The Human Predicament,* David Benatar, is a professor of

Philosophy at the University of Cape Town, obviously a learned person who has devoted his life to the study and teaching of philosophy.

In her well written review, Ms. Bourke notes that Professor Benatar is "merciless in spelling out his message," which is that our lives are meaningless, that evolution (which of course they would agree is a fact) is blind and serves no intrinsic purpose, and that in a cosmic sense each of us lives for only an insignificant amount of time. Apparently he does maintain that humans can enjoy "terrestrial meanings," by doing such things as rearing children, helping refugees, composing a symphony or making a meal.

Ms. Bourke polled a number of her friends, and none of them believed there is some wider purpose to human existence. She believes "cosmic meaningfulness" is irrelevant and claims that recognizing that our lives lack "cosmic meaning" is liberating. In her book she coined the term "negative zoology, a celebration of life that is always unstable and indeterminate." It understands the desire for meaning, but maintains that is impossible. Well, if you start out with the premise that it's impossible, it's a sure bet you will never discover it, right?

And that's the way it is with many of our scientists and thinkers. I have the greatest respect for their intellects and their ability to study vast amounts of input, analyze it all and come up with conclusions in their scholarly works. But I could never understand how they disregard the solid evidence cited in this and my earlier books. Certainly in the case of the author and reviewer mentioned above, their field is focused on the meaning of human existence, so of course they'd look for any evidence they could find to indicate it might have meaning, right?

How could they ignore the input of all those dead airmen who died in the R-101 as recently as 1930? Their studies span the ages, so they'd have to be aware of something so relatively current, wouldn't they? Is it possible they never heard of Edgar Cayce? And how about Betty White's input to her husband in 1939? Are they not aware of these documented events and related information? Do they just ignore them? Perhaps they automatically exclude from their awareness any information that comes to us through psychics and mediums, believing it is impossible for that to occur and that any medium is by their very nature a fraud or a fool.

Again, it is difficult for me to understand why they won't even investigate it. Why are they so willing to give credence to the musings of humans who are alive in their bodies, with obviously limited intellects and knowledge, while they absolutely refuse to give any credence to entities who have passed on and could conceivably have access to much greater intelligences that are not living in a human body at the time they communicate? Why do they assume that any personality who survives what we call death could not have any strong motives for coming back to tell us what our and their larger existence is like? Or once again, do they just assume that is impossible, and let it go at that.

According to my sources, we will all eventually learn "the way things really are" at some point after we die and before our "next" incarnation. So we'll all be okay. But the big downside of living a life with the belief system of the good professors is that, as Ms. Bourke stated at the start of her review, "there are books that one should never give to depressed friends." Indeed, it is only natural to wonder from time to time just what our fate and our meaning is. Their belief system casts a pall over life that would be difficult for many to overcome by adopting the "negative zoology" philosophy.

I am not a learned professor, and it's likely you aren't either if you're reading such a simple book as this. But consider all the evidence provided by personalities in spirit form who were respected while they were alive on earth. They had good reason and good intentions to communicate information they considered important and helpful to many of those alive in bodies. When you look at the sum total of their communications, it's likely you will come to the conclusion that indeed they are valid sources of information, and they had a lot of beneficial information to share with us.

So if for the moment, for the sake of doing some creative thinking and reasoning, you can put doubts aside and agree that this might truly be the way things are, the question arises, does it make any difference? How might life be different in this 21st century if we all understood that we are essentially spirits, and that all the material things around us that seem so solid and independent of us, are in fact our own creations and under our control?

In the following chapters we'll take a look at some of the ways things might change drastically – all for the better. These are my inferences and guesses. Yours might be different. But at the very least a discussion of these issues will set us all to thinking. And thoughts, remember, have their own reality that, according to my belief system, will find expression somewhere. If that's so, then these thoughts might find expression in the reality some of us experience in the years ahead. That's reason enough to devote some further thinking to this question.

Chapter 5 - Do Scientists Agree With Any of This?

"Scientists" is a term that covers a lot of people. Certainly many of them would consider all of this rubbish, and they'd be scornful of anyone who would be foolish enough to believe anything that supposedly is communicated by a medium from a dead person. Even bothering to consider such information would be a waste of time as they see it. But there is one group that has come to some conclusions very similar to what spirit entities have told us – quantum physicists.

In earlier books I summarized 40 relevant theories of quantum physicists, many of which had been demonstrated in laboratory tests. They were taken from two books published in the 1980s, *The Dancing Wu Li Masters* by Gary Zukav and *The Tao of Physics* by Fritjof Capra. These books were published over 30 years ago and I haven't bothered to keep up with the latest theories in physics, but to my knowledge none of those 40 has been refuted.

It is doubtful these scientists were trying to prove anything "spiritual" or even to confirm the existence of spirits. They were just relating either the results of their experiments or their theories based on what they had observed. Here are some of those results and theories that seem to agree with what dead people have told us.

- When you investigate how things happen in the world of the smallest elements of matter, the things that happen contradict common sense.

- It is not possible to observe reality without changing it.

- There is not necessarily an objective reality out there apart from our experience of it.

- Sub-atomic particles seem to know instantaneously what decisions are made elsewhere, even as far away as another galaxy, and they instantly act on the information – so they might very well be living particles, evaluating and acting on information as we do.

- The wave function, which represents all possibilities that might happen to anything when it interacts with an observer, is not just a mathematical fiction, but a real thing, and all the possibilities happen. They all actualize in different worlds that co-exist with ours.

- Experience tells us the physical world is solid, real and independent of us, but this is simply not so.

- There might well be no valid distinction between what is "in here" (in our minds) and "out there" (the world outside of us).

- What we experience is not external reality, but our interaction with it. The world consists not of things, but of interactions.

- Without us, the entire world we interact with does not exist. We are the creators of the universe.

- The existence of one ultimate flow of time throughout the physical universe is an incorrect perception.

- Time and space are not separate. There is only one space-time, a continuum that flows continuously. It is more useful to think in terms of a static, nonmoving picture of space in time, in which events just are, as opposed to a view in which time moves forward and events develop. Events do not develop, they just are.

- All the past, present and future exist at once, and for each individual they meet and forever meet at one single point ... now.

- There is no such thing as matter. It is a curvature of the space-time continuum. Matter is actually a series of patterns out of focus. The search for the ultimate stuff of the universe ends with the discovery that there isn't any.

- The world is fundamentally dancing energy. Physical reality is essentially non-substantial. Matter is simply the momentary manifestation of interacting fields.

- Movements backward and forward in time are no more significant than movements backward and forward in space.

- There are particle interactions in which, where there was nothing, in a flash, particles come into being, then vanish without a trace. This shows the concept of a completely empty, barren "space" is simply a notion we have made up. There is no such thing as empty space.

- We have lived so long in our abstractions that instead of realizing they are drawn *from* the real world, we believe they *are* the real world.

- The most fundamental level of reality is an unbroken wholeness, which is "that-which-is." It denies the idea that we can analyze the world along the lines of separately and independently existing parts.

- Both being and "non-being" are "that-which-is." Everything, even emptiness, is "that which is." There is nothing which is not "that which is."

These theorems and conclusions have many similarities to what respected dead people have told us. This includes the nature of illusions and matter, our perception of time, how we perceive things while in the physical body, the existence of probable realities and more. A logical conclusion is that some scientists have indeed agreed with some of what dead people have told us. Correct or not, the parallels are remarkable.

Chapter 6 – Implications for Major Science-Based Fields

When thinking about science as we know it, we need to remember that scientists in a variety of fields have made life much better for us by using their method of inspecting, analyzing and manipulating matter that they assume is both real and separate from them.

Consider almost any field of activity that affects humanity in big ways and you will quickly see that this is so. Medicine and healthcare, transportation, aviation and space travel, agriculture, energy, physical hygiene, communications, weather forecasting – the evidence is abundant.

The problem is, **the more these scientists focus intently on the world of matter and how to manipulate it to our physical advantage, the more difficult it becomes for them to ever discover that the world of matter itself is just a useful illusion under our control.**

Thinking about this, the image comes to mind of a fly buzzing around a television screen showing a recently baked apple pie. Buzz as it might, gathering whatever input it can from the screen, that fly will never have the slightest clue as to what an apple pie really is or what it tastes or smells like. Neither will it ever guess the existence of a technology that makes it possible for that image to appear.

By their own measure they are doing quite well, so

why would any of these scientists ever consider that they have devoted their lifetimes and their considerable talents and intellects to manipulating something that is just an illusion? If I were in their situation, I certainly wouldn't. But for all their progress, what might happen if somehow they did? How might we be better off?

Space Travel

Our nation spends a lot of time, talent and energy on space travel. The goal is to send huge payloads of physical material and perhaps humans as well to other planets. It seems to be a reasonable goal that might pay off in the very long term. But the cost is huge, and there are many other things we might spend the money on, such as eradicating disease, eliminating hunger and providing decent housing for those who don't have it now.

What if we could make space travel dramatically more cost efficient? Might we not achieve our goals more quickly while making it possible for some of the dollars expended to be put to other good uses?

When Bob Monroe had his group of "explorers," gifted psychics, set out to explore the other planets, it quickly became boring, since they perceived essentially what our astronauts did – rocky barren landscapes. (Though some theorists suspect the astronauts also reported UFOs about 15,000 feet above them in space, observing them.)

When the "explorers" started using an affirmation, however, one that requested the assistance of any intelligences of good intent whose wisdom and knowledge were equal to or greater than their own, they began to make contact with spirit beings whose intelligence was clearly many magnitudes greater than ours. The explorers' purposes, and Bob's purposes during many subsequent journeys he took with such beings, did not involve space travel as we think of it.

But let's consider their findings before they started to make such contact. Using their non-matter consciousness, they actually saw the terrain. Imagine how helpful it would be if all they did was to act as scouts for the astronauts who would eventually travel to these planets in physical form. They could identify the best places to land, areas where the soil most closely resembles earth, dangerous areas to avoid, etc.

Now imagine if a group of talented people started to use their consciousness to inquire of more enlightened beings how we earthlings might best advance our sciences to accelerate our efforts in this area. Certainly there are discoveries yet to be made in materials science, propulsion and extension of human life spans, that these intelligences might share with us, saving trillions of dollars and hastening by centuries our ability to travel to and perhaps colonize other planets.

If we made a lot of progress along these lines, we might decide it is wiser to travel with just our consciousnesses until we have learned a great deal that way, before we start to spend enormous sums on exploring with material spaceships in our physical bodies. We might, for example, get guidance on the best planets to colonize and how best to adapt our physical bodies to the environment on a given planet.

Now consider the return on investment of our space programs, not just for the United States, but for any other countries exploring space. Talented psychics traveling with their consciousness might be able to suggest avoiding some planets altogether and focusing only on those holding the most promise. Imagine how many taxpayer dollars could be saved!

But the possibilities go well beyond dollars and cents. These explorers would not be limited to just our solar system. They could travel with their consciousness to virtually anywhere in the galaxy or the trillions of other galaxies, and they could complete that travel instantly. Since consciousness travel appears to take no time at all, we wouldn't have to wait centuries for them to travel to other planets in other galaxies and come back with any information they might gather.

Remember, they could experience other planets with perception capabilities no greater than the astronauts, or they could choose to seek out intelligent species, who might guide and instruct them so they gain the most knowledge and experience possible. Then, like Bob Monroe, they could immediately travel "back to earth" and inform us about all the exciting experiences, ideas, guidance and instruction they received. Some of that information might even enable us humans to make "quantum leaps" in physical space travel, with means of propulsion we only dream of now, or can't even imagine.

Given what Bob Monroe's explorers learned with only a small dedicated effort by a few people, imagine what might be learned and discovered with a large, well-funded program that would cost only a tiny fraction of what we're currently spending on space exploration. We're talking here about consciousness exploration under the guidance and direction of scientists who are seeking greater benefits for our material earth civilization.

Or perhaps we'd opt for the methods used by souls who still visit earth around the year 3000 when Bob Monroe, escorted by intelligent spirits, traveled to one probable version of earth at that time. Apparently they created bodies when they wanted them out of the available earth materials, without the need for the birthing process. Or they could temporarily enter one of the physical bodies that might be lying in storage in protected cocoons. You might remember, Bob was informed that one of their main purposes for visiting earth at that time was to join their consciousness with various species, so they'd know what a fish, a leaf, a panther, etc., experiences during earth life.

Regardless of what we choose to do with the information imparted to us, and perhaps with any talents that advanced intelligences help us develop, it is quite likely our travels through the universe would be far speedier, more productive, instructive and cost efficient if we devote a portion of our expenditures to traveling with just our consciousness first, before attempting physical travel.

When you consider the potential payoff and the low cost, it makes sense for scientists to systematically research how these abilities might be harnessed to our practical benefit right here and now. If they would just take the time to review the evidence that suggests this could be a significant source of beneficial input, they might decide it makes sense to at least take the first few steps toward using directed consciousness research.

Medicine

The pace of progress in medicine today is breathtaking. Medical instruments can view, analyze and mend body parts that weren't accessible a decade ago. Telemedicine enables physicians to diagnose and recommend treatment for patients a great distance from them. Detailed knowledge of our DNA and methods for modifying it promise breakthroughs in prevention of serious diseases and disorders. And recently CAR-T treatment, where specially designed cells were used to treat pediatric leukemia patients to achieve 90% remission rates, was approved by an advisory committee of the Food & Drug Administration. Progress seems to be coming faster, and in more varied fields of medicine.

It is exciting and encouraging to see all the advances being made in medicine, not just in gene research and editing to treat previously untreatable diseases, but also in new micro-instruments that can perform single-port surgery that is much less invasive, in diet and nutrition, in the application of sound, electromagnetic fields and many other areas.

Now consider the possibility that many prominent leading medical researchers and doctors who have "died" in the last few decades continued their development in the "pure spirit" stage between lives. Further assume they could communicate with us on earth through respected mediums to impart knowledge about medical developments in our future, so that we could pull these developments into our present on an accelerated basis. As an analogy, if we're already advancing in medical science at the rate of 100 miles per hour, perhaps we could accelerate to 1000 miles per hour with the help of spirits who intend to incarnate in our future as leading medical personalities.

In science fiction and in Edgar Cayce's visits to Atlantis, mention is often made of therapies making use of crystals, sound frequencies, electricity and light that healed people from all sorts of illnesses and physical defects. Indeed, in our own current medical community, many of these are already put to good use daily, as scientists discover the power of different modalities for healing, including sound, electromagnetism and various frequencies of light. Why not use the proven abilities of some of us for communicating with advanced spirits who are motivated to help us accelerate our efforts in all aspects of healing, including our current basic methods of drugs and surgery, but extending far beyond them?

Now imagine if our leading scientists in the various medical fields could have access to advanced intelligences. They could learn of cures in a matter of days that might otherwise have taken years to discover. Therapies that make use of light, sound, electromagnetism and electricity were apparently used in technologically advanced civilizations of the distant past. They could be rediscovered and applied in the next few decades.

Our medical scientists are in the initial stages of using these technologies, and have been applying some of them for decades. So we have the medically knowledgeable scientists who would be capable of learning and applying whatever advanced intelligences would care to share with us. We could leapfrog through various stages of progress and enjoy the benefits of advanced treatments in mere months or years, instead of waiting for slow progress over decades.

As with space travel, the cost would be inconsequential compared to what we spend on medical research now, and the payoff might be far larger than any of us could imagine.

Power of the Mind

And all of those scientific advances would pale in comparison to the ultimate promise of consciousness applied to healing. Years ago, in a book titled *Remarkable Recoveries,* there were a number of anecdotes about people recovering from illnesses by the power of their minds. One case that was especially instructive involved a man seriously ill who was told by his doctor that a new treatment had just become available and the man rapidly improved when it was administered.

He then read in the paper that it was not as effective as originally promised, and he immediately regressed. Then the doctor told him that was a mistake, that it was really effective, and he improved immediately. This demonstrated, along with many other stories, that the mind and its beliefs can control the health of the physical body.

Several studies have supported this contention. Bernie Siegel MD, in *Love, Medicine & Miracles* and other books, cited many examples of people who visualized their way to recovery from various illnesses, including cancer, by using imaging techniques to envision, for example, a tumor shrinking or cancer cells dying off or converting to healthy cells.

And of course, we have the phenomenon of the placebo effect, where people believing they are getting a drug that will cure them but are actually getting only a sugar pill, recover. This phenomenon is so prevalent that for drugs to be proven effective they must exceed the effectiveness of the placebo effect, which in some cases can result in as many as 20% of patients recovering or improving.

None of these examples are conclusive, of course, but certainly they warrant extensive study of how consciousness can bring about improvements, remissions and cures using no material methods. Consider the billions that have been devoted to cancer research over the decades. If just a fraction of that amount had been devoted to researching how consciousness can bring about medical progress, it is quite possible it would be considered part of standard procedures for patients with many serious illnesses. The material therapies and treatments would still be predominant of course, but even if applied consciousness is used only to supplement the material treatments of drugs and surgeries, the results might be dramatic.

Of course, as long as scientists rule out even the possibility of using expansion of our consciousness to connect with non-material intelligences or to heal ourselves with our minds, none of this will ever happen. Perhaps the recent experience of scientists experimenting with the Hadron Collider will persuade them to change their minds. Those scientists learned to their surprise that they as observers could affect the sub-microscopic particles they were experimenting with.

They might not have been so surprised if they had read the 1972 best seller *The Secret Life of Plants,* where among many other experiments recounted, they would learn about Ingo Swann, an out-of-body traveler, who was able to affect a mechanism in Stanford University's most thoroughly shielded "quark" chamber, buried deep underground in a vault of liquid helium, impenetrable to any known wavelength of the electromagnetic spectrum. Around 1970 Seth mentioned that scientists were just discovering that their thoughts and emotions could affect matter, but they have yet to realize that they create it.

Energy

A recent television episode of "Ancient Aliens" focusing on their technologies speculated on the possibility that some ancient civilizations were able to move massive boulders weighing many tons by using special sounds and sound frequencies. This would be consistent with what the entity Seth described in some of his sessions when he spoke through Jane Roberts, describing what some ancient civilizations, which existed on this planet long before ours did, were capable of.

When the episode focused on the amount of currently existing machinery that would be required to duplicate some of the ancient stonework used to build massive walls, stadiums and other structures, it estimated the cost and effort would be huge, if in fact such structures could be built at all in some of the remote regions where these were located.

Perhaps no aspect of our world economy in 2017 has been the focus of so much attention as energy. Oil prices, refinery capacity, shipping for both transportation and storage, China requiring that electricity should become the major energy source for powering cars within its borders, OPEC production cutbacks, nuclear reactors and their peaceful as well as military applications, hydrogen powered vehicles, solar panels and their evolving technologies, wind power, the impact of natural gas on coal and other fuels – the list goes on and on. Every day there are feature articles in major publications and television shows on the popular channels dedicated to some aspect of energy developments. Many focus on the future of various energy sources, whether and how they should be regulated, and whether governments need to establish policies to limit or stimulate them.

It is an exciting time for energy developments on our planet right now. And how much more exciting might these times be if we also had input right now from those in pure spirit form. They might inform us about energy sources related to sound, to crystals, to safe forms of nuclear energy if there are any, and even to the use of our own minds to create energy via intense concentration.

Bob Monroe, when he traveled to one probability of the year 3000, witnessed entities who got all the energy they needed to sustain themselves just by stretching out their arms and "tuning in" to the energies surrounding the earth. We've only just begun to explore the possibilities of electromagnetism and how it affects our planet. Given the possibility that ancient civilizations did in fact move huge multi-ton stones with just sound, as even some scientists are now theorizing according to TV documentaries, that might be a particularly promising energy source to explore. Imagine the cost efficiency and the environmental benefits if, instead of using huge machinery and consuming a lot of fossil fuels, we could build structures using only sound to transport, lift and place heavy materials, regardless of whether the location is in the middle of a bustling city or in remote forests and mountains.

To my knowledge there is no serious research being conducted on this possibility, and there is not likely to be, given the bias of the scientific community against considering any input from spirit as worthwhile or relevant. But is it possible, a phrase the TV documentaries use frequently, that if we were to make contact with spirit entities we might discover how to create and apply the kind of sound described by the Seth entity? When you weigh the potential benefits, it seems it would be worth a try, especially considering the low cost of doing so.

Sound is not the only potential beneficial technology of course. Nicola Tesla, who claimed to receive information for his many inventions from extraterrestrial (as in spirit) sources, built a tower on Long Island, NY that sent electricity through the air. He was intent on finding a way to provide free energy for everyone on the planet. His financial backer, however, who was tied to energy that people had to pay for, is said to have pulled his support because he and others could make a fortune by having people pay for energy that Tesla might otherwise provide for free.

Whether or not that is the case, it is tantalizing to think about how electromagnetism or some other energy source already abundant on our planet might be harnessed for use by almost anyone at little or no cost. Benevolent spirits, of course, if they were guiding us, would surely recommend the safest and most environmentally friendly ways to apply such energy.

Weather Forecasting and Climate Change

The year 2017 was one that saw billions of dollars' worth of damage caused by hurricanes, floods, fires, drought, tornadoes and other weather-related disasters. It was also a year in which the debates about climate change became ever more intense.

Consider the benefits if, following advice from spirit intelligences, we were able to discover ways to forecast weather occurrences far more precisely than we do now. Or even, perhaps, if we learned new methods to modify and control weather patterns, so that some of the disasters would never occur. Again, you can only imagine the cynicism and mockery that would prevail on the part of the scientific community if spirit contact were ever suggested.

On the other hand, since so many scientific advances were discovered "by accident" or after someone had taken a nap or wakened from a dream, might some scientists make the connection that there is a real possibility the breakthroughs were received in some state of consciousness other than our normal focus on the "real world" around us, in other words, from non-material or spirit consciousness?

If they were to make that connection and devote just a tiny portion of their time and assets to exploring what we might learn about the weather, who knows what we might find out? Could it be that intense storms are partially created by our minds and emotions, as Seth maintained, functioning as a release of tensions that would otherwise drive us mad? Could we learn how to use the power of our thoughts and emotions to impact the weather substantially? Might we discover or rediscover that certain materials or laser rays might be used to moderate weather events or change their course?

Logically it would make sense that actions such as these are not impossible. In fact, variations of some of these ideas have already been tried by human scientists. With guidance from spirit intelligences we might develop effective technologies to deal with weather disasters decades or centuries sooner than we might otherwise. It would cost so little and mean so much.

Climate Change

And what about the hot-button issue of our early 21st century world, climate change? On the one hand a group of scientists are urgently warning us that unless we change our fuel sources, or even if we do, we are in for perilous climate changes in the next hundred years or so, and they label anyone who disagrees with them as "climate deniers."

On the other side are a group of scientists who claim that the first group has intentionally biased its research to support their scenario, ignoring many facts that would disprove it and using algorithms that are faulty in order to come to preconceived conclusions. They claim that the first group would cause untold economic damage to most of the world's economies if their recommendations were implemented

I don't know enough to have a strong opinion one way or the other. I suppose I'd have more confidence in the climate change scientists if they hadn't changed their theme from global warming to climate change, in order to account for a recent string of successive years when the temperature was lower than they anticipated. Regardless, while I don't know enough to favor a particular set of recommended actions …. Spirit intelligences might.

With their awareness of the probable futures we might experience if we implemented one or another set of actions, the odds are good that they could guide us along paths that would lead to ideal climate developments in the century ahead.

Transportation

One of the big questions of the early 21st century is whether electric vehicles will replace gas-powered ones. Many industry experts and futurists predict they will, perhaps as early as 2030. Others are not so sure, citing a number of practical obstacles. It is an interesting debate, but I sure wish it were about more than just electric vs gasoline. The physicist Michio Kaku claims that hydrogen-powered vehicles offer a better alternative, since hydrogen is plentiful and the exhaust is non-polluting water. There are many technical hurdles to be overcome, but some large companies are working on overcoming them.

You have to wonder, though, if we could tap into the knowledge of spirit intelligences, whether we might learn about other sources, perhaps even more plentiful, with fewer technology challenges, and available at very low cost or no cost at all. Scientists are well aware of the electromagnetic energy grid surrounding earth and the fact that some geographic coordinates have stronger energy than others. Seth gave some information about this, naming areas of the United States where more energy is available, which he said helps people in those areas to manifest their ideas more effectively than those in other areas.

A number of scientists did confer with Seth in sessions with Jane Roberts, but these are not published to my knowledge. (Most scientists would understandably be concerned if it ever became known in their professional community that they had consulted a psychic.) Consider for a moment, though, if scientists with a specific mission in mind – harnessing the energy grid to propel land, air and undersea vehicles – succeeded in making contact with spirit intelligences that could instruct them on how to make that happen. What a difference that might make in solving all our energy challenges here on earth!

We'd have an abundant, virtually infinite, non-polluting source of power for the entire planet, at low or no cost. As long as some of us don't decide to get in the way and start charging others large sums for the energy, speedy progress by even poor nations might be possible in solving their challenges related not just to transportation, but to providing clean water and power for all their inhabitants.

The electromagnetic grid might not be the only invisible source of energy. It's just one scientists are already aware of. Perhaps there are others as yet undiscovered, that are even more powerful and more easily adapted to our needs. Communications with spirit entities motivated to help us might accelerate discovery of such energy sources, as well as the best methods for controlling and applying them to make possible totally new means of powering all modes of transportation.

Agriculture

Anyone who reads the 1972 best seller, *The Secret Life of Plants* by Peter Tompkins and Christopher Bird, is presented with reams of solid evidence that plants and trees have consciousness, and are even capable of reading our minds. The most dramatic example which became widely known was when Cleve Backster in 1966 attached the electrodes of a lie detector to the leaves of his office plant, to see if they responded to different stimuli.

The moment he thought of burning a leaf to which the electrodes were attached and pictured the flame in his mind, the plant registered a strong reaction. When he returned with matches the plant registered another surge. When he actually burned the leaf, there was a lower peak of reaction. Later when he went through the motions of pretending to burn another leaf, but really had no intention of doing so, there was no reaction. What happened? There could be many explanations, *but one logical conclusion is that the plant somehow was able to know the difference between a real intent to burn a leaf, and just pretending.*

Subsequent experiments showed that plants reacted not just to immediate threats of harm, but also anticipated threats, such as a dog in the room, or the appearance of a person who might do them harm. On one occasion a Canadian physiologist visited Backster, whose plants reacted in a strange way. Backster then asked the physiologist if any part of his work involved harming plants. It turns out that *he regularly killed plants, put them in an oven and roasted them to find out their dry weight.*

Another relatively simple but compelling example of the power of thoughts and the existence of a spirit world that underlies our physical one, is what Marcel Vogel was able to achieve. Vogel was a research chemist working with IBM in Los Gatos CA, who had previously studied for years to become a Franciscan priest. When he learned of Backster's experiments, he decided to conduct experiments of his own on plants. He was successful in duplicating some of Backster's results, but the three teams of his students were totally unsuccessful.

That set him to wondering about the existence of "psychic energy" in certain chemicals and how that energy might be stored. He approached a spiritually gifted friend, Vivian Wiley, who told him that working with the chemicals would not help him discover anything, and they agreed that she could experiment with energy focused on plants without any chemicals. She picked two leaves from a saxifrage plant in her garden, and for a month she focused each day on one, willing it to live, while she ignored the other. After a month, the ignored leaf was beginning to decay, while the leaf she had focused on was healthy and green, as though it had been freshly picked.

Vogel decided to see if he could get similar results. He picked three elm leaves, put them on a glass plate, and each day concentrated on the two outer leaves, projecting loving feelings and encouraging them to live, while ignoring the center leaf. After just a week the center leaf had shriveled, while the outer leaves were not only still green, but it appeared the severed stems had healed the wounds caused when they were ripped from the tree.

Vogel was an expert in liquid crystals, on which he had worked and researched for IBM. After viewing extensively liquid crystal behavior under a microscope, he concluded that crystals are brought into a solid (physical) state by "pre-forms," similar to "ghost images" of pure energy, which anticipate the existence of the solids. In his subsequent experiments with plants, he found that fleshy leaves with high water content reacted to human thoughts and emotions more than other leaves, and individual leaves seemed to have their own unique "personality."

These are just a few of dozens of examples presented in *Secret Life* that show that plants and trees have consciousness. That book and many others describe the ability of George Washington Carver, a leading agricultural chemist who was born a slave, to communicate with plants, which always responded positively to him. He is perhaps most remembered for introducing the peanut to southern farmers and creating dozens of products from it, so that it became a valuable cash crop. He also instructed the farmers how to replenish their soil which had gradually become less fertile through repeated plantings of a single crop, cotton.

It is interesting to note that Carver, when questioned about his abilities, claimed that nature was the best teacher, and that in the early morning hours before sunrise, God would tell him about the plans he was to fulfill. Whether those messages came directly from God or from a benevolent spirit intent on helping humans, Carver apparently used his listening abilities to create a lifetime of achievements related to agriculture, which ultimately helped millions. Answering a puzzled observer, he explained that the secrets were in the plants, that you could learn them if you loved the plants enough, and anyone was capable of doing what he did.

Another well-known phenomenon addressed in *Secret Life* is Findhorn. In a barren coastal area in northern Scotland, where poor soil and strong winds had apparently made it almost impossible to grow anything, some psychically gifted people succeeded in growing a wide variety of strong, healthy and large vegetables. Those people were led to that particular place in visions they had while in a clairvoyant state. Their unexplained success soon became widely known, and the area was eventually populated by a variety of spiritual seekers.

In the United States there is a garden in Virginia named Perelandra created by Machaelle Small Wright, who has also achieved remarkable results with vegetables and flowers, witnessed by thousands who have toured Perelandra. She has psychic abilities and attributes her garden achievements to her ability to communicate with devas, the animating spirit of various plants at the "architect" level, as well as "nature spirits" which do the detailed and continuing work of taking a concept from the spiritual level to the physical. They can appear to some people as gnomes and fairies, she said, but they appear to her as bodies of light energy. In 1981 she wrote a book about her experiences titled *Behaving as if the God in all Life Mattered,* and updated it in 1997. She has also written *Dancing in the Shadows of the Moon* and other books, where she related other experiences.

She is a very impressive person with a keen intellect who survived a difficult childhood and became a stronger person in the process. In her first book she shared that she had been coached by spirit entities, devas and nature spirits to develop the ability to manifest seeds and garden tools. This is not manifesting as it is often referred to, meaning focusing intently on something you want so that it eventually comes into your life, such as focusing on a new bicycle and then getting one as a gift from a totally unexpected source. Rather, she actually made objects materialize physically where there was previously nothing there except air, along the lines of Christ's "miracle of the loaves and fishes."

Given her interests and priorities, the first thing she manifested was a cubic foot of manure, and then she progressed to seeds and the garden tools. This is remarkable to me, as I am not aware of any other person in modern western civilization who claims to be able to do this, but admittedly I have not researched the subject. This is extremely significant because it is this ability to create physically what we imagine that will, according to the Seth entity, bring about almost unimaginable advances for the human race, as discussed in depth in *The 2075 Movement.*

In fact, she would have been included in the chapter on living people with unusual talents, except for the fact that, given her values and priorities, she refuses to demonstrate her abilities, which means there is no physical evidence to support her claims. She refuses for what I consider excellent reasons. The believers would say it's not necessary to prove anything, she states, those on the fence would want continuing exhibitions of ever larger objects, and the skeptics would accuse her of being a fraud. She has no time for such distractions, and has other things she wants to achieve with her ability to manifest.

It is interesting that Joe McMoneagle, on the other hand, has been willing to demonstrate his unusual abilities many times in public. Here we would do well to remember that each person has his or her own priorities and goals. Despite the lack of physical evidence, Machaelle Small Wright shares details of what she experienced when manifesting that correspond closely to what the entity Seth described in explaining how physical matter is formed from "electromagnetic energy units," or EEUs. There are differences, of course, since one is experiencing and the other is describing, but there are similarities, especially in the slowing down of frequencies. In fact, much of what she experienced firsthand agrees in principle with many of the main points in this book, with respect to spirit being the source of matter.

Another reputable person who has communicated with devas and written about it is Meredith Young Sowers. A humorous incident was included in her first edition of *Agartha*. Meredith had developed psychic abilities while attending a session at *The Monroe Institute* in Faber VA and later established *Stillpoint* in Walpole NH, centered on energy healing. When she discovered she could communicate with the devas of various vegetables she had planted in her garden, she would occasionally meditate there and ask them if they had anything to communicate to her.

On one occasion the "spirit of the peas" asked her to be still for a few minutes and then describe what she experienced. She did so and had a very unpleasant feeling which involved swaying and feeling a bit nauseous. When she informed the "spirit of the peas" that she didn't like the feeling at all, it replied "Neither do we." The deva then asked her to attach the vine more firmly to the fence, so it would no longer have to frequently sway in the breeze.

Given such dramatic evidence provided by respectable, level-headed people who achieved such impressive results, it would seem worthwhile to devote substantial sums and energies to communication with spirit intelligences that apparently stand ready to help us if we reach out to them. At the very least we could expect to gain valuable insights about soil, pesticides, plants that can revitalize soil, earthworms and other organisms living in the soil, and how to grow food in mediums other than soil, a field that has already gained traction but is still in its infancy.

Chapter 7 – Implications for Major Issues of Our Time

We have a lot going on around our planet these days. We have all kinds of issues to deal with. To keep it simple, though, I am going to put them in just three categories – world peace, personal happiness and "the end of....", meaning the end of a whole bucketful of negatives that we don't seem to be dealing with too well right now.

World Peace

Imagine if Vladimir Putin in Russia, Xi Jinping in China, the Ayatollah in Iran, Kim Jong Un in North Korea, Raul Castro in Cuba, Nicolas Maduro in Venezuela and several other South America dictators of his ilk all realized that every one of us is essentially a spirit temporarily in physical form. Imagine if they all knew that the physical world is actually an illusion we are using to help us develop our full capabilities as spirits.

Imagine too that they all knew that most of us spirits come into many different bodies in various lifetimes, playing many different roles that might range from itinerant beggar woman to powerful king, to successful businessperson to poor migrant worker and more, in many cultures and races – and that all of them are going on right now simultaneously!

Do you think any of them would suppress millions of people, kill or turn into refugees millions more, cause starvation and focus only on more power, wealth and physical comforts for themselves as they do now? It just wouldn't make sense. When you know the truth about the Human Time-Space Illusion, and that your purpose for coming in to play the game is to become aware that we are powerful spirits who create what we experience through the power of our own thoughts and emotions, why would any of them do anything but try to provide the best possible life for all those they govern?

They'd understand that in their present roles they have the opportunity to either make huge strides in their goal to fulfill in the physical world their very best values as spirits, or they could take many steps backward by using their free will to act as they do now, fostering hatred, disease, oppression, starvation and wars. Logic is on the side of their acting quite differently from their present courses of action. They are all intelligent and would all immediately realize that what they perceive now as winning is really losing … in a very big way.

They wouldn't want to suppress their own people or declare war on others. Selfishly, and selfish is okay, they'd want to take whatever steps they could to make sure as many of their people as possible realized their own power to create the world they want to experience, without needing to take anything from any other person. Could world peace be very far behind?

Personal Happiness for Everyone

Despite all the tumult around the globe, many of us succeed in achieving some measure of personal happiness

94

when we and our families are in good health, with plenty to eat, interesting and enjoyable things to do, some good friends to share experiences with and plenty to laugh about. Of course, right now a lot of people do not have those circumstances. Many still manage to find a measure of happiness when they deal effectively with big challenges such as disease, a major disability, a severe accident, loss of a loved one or disappointment in their career. That still leaves many who don't deal so effectively with these challenges, and many more around the globe who eke out a meager existence, perhaps going hungry most days, or perhaps having to work to exhaustion just to survive. They have few reasons to be happy.

But now consider how different their circumstances might be once they discover they are actually powerful spirits who can control and direct their thoughts and emotions to create a physical world of abundance and joy. Even if they can't do that immediately, once they realized this and started on a path to develop those abilities, they'd have the satisfaction of knowing that each day they are getting closer to their full potential, where they can at will create an enjoyable life full of personal happiness. However long the development process might take, months or years if necessary, they'd have the anticipation of experiencing that enjoyable world, which would add some measure of personal happiness even if they're not quite there yet.

Remember, according to various sources mentioned earlier, after we escape the limits imposed by being in a physical body and expand our conscious awareness (commonly referred to now as death), most of go through various stages of development and training for our further advancement as spirits.

One of those stages is what Bob Monroe called the Belief System Territories, where the inhabitants know they can create all sorts of joyful experiences and surroundings just by thinking about them. Apparently, as noted earlier, many of them stay in that stage for hundreds of our years, believing it to be the Heaven of our current beliefs, before they move on to more advanced stages.

Well, personal happiness here on earth for everyone would not be all that different from the Belief System Territories, once we understand the full extent of our being and the powers we possess. We'd each have our own individual version of our ideal world, and that's fine, because your version of what you experience does not have to interact with or affect mine. Remember, there are as many different versions of the pretty girl entering a room as there are people observing her.

The End Of …

Choose your favorite that you'd like to see no more of. Fear, hunger, stress, war and killing, brutal dictatorships, disease, scarcity, famine, pestilence, jealousy, envy, hatred, bullying, race wars, greed, excessive pride and thinking you're better than others, unemployment and boredom, loneliness and isolation.

None of them will be around once we recognize that we are spirits, and that the physical world is merely the

96

result of our thoughts and emotions being projected in the Human Time-Space Illusion, giving us feedback so we can continually develop our ability to create in ways that are most beneficial and enjoyable to ourselves and others.

Ourselves and others? Are they really different? Maybe, but once we know that as observers we not only affect the world we experience, but also create it by virtue of our own construction of ideas about reality, we are likely to discover, as some have maintained, that there is at the very least a cosmic web of connections that bind us all. We might even discover that, at a level we can't perceive right now, we are all united as one. What does that do to the concept of aggressively waging war and killing large numbers of fellow humans, as Putin was willing to do when he invaded Ukraine?

It is true that in World War II the United States as a nation felt forced to participate in war after we were attacked at Pearl Harbor. At the level of our spiritual development then, which is about the same as it is now, we didn't seem to have another realistic option to stop the killing and bring about peace. But assume for a moment that we develop enough by 2075, as Seth predicted, so that we can experience and feel our connection to other humans, and indeed, to all of creation. Would we be able to join our minds with those of attackers and influence them so that they become peaceful, as apparently some "holy men" in remote parts of our planet can do?

That might not be so far-fetched as you might think. Marcel Vogel, who was mentioned earlier, succeeded as far back as the 1970s in teaching children to unite their consciousness with plants, (just as Bob Monroe experienced when he traveled in time to a version of our earth around the year 3000). Not long afterward another scientifically trained researcher, Pierre Paul Sauvin from West Paterson NJ, was able to do the same thing. He went even further by demonstrating before large audiences that he could make a toy train reverse direction merely by directing intense thoughts at a plant that was wired to the train track. He later learned he could do this sort of thing even from great distances, such as his holiday cabin 80 miles away in New York State. His achievements, like Vogel's, are detailed in *The Secret Life of Plants*.

So can we look forward to the day when even excitable and dangerous dictators like Kim Jong Un in North Korea are turned into peaceful, loving characters by lots of us sending the right kind of mental messages and emotions to him? We're not there yet at our present level of development, but if we could do that, while he also comes to realize that he and everyone else is a spirit, and that we are all connected, who knows what kind of positive, peaceful actions might result?

Right now he feels himself separate from, and superior to, all the people he is killing and imprisoning in labor camps, but when he realizes his is just one role of many that he's playing, he'd have a hard time continuing to fear what these people might do if they were free to live their lives as they please. In fact, with those realizations, each one of us would have a difficult time maintaining an emotion of anger, jealousy, greed or hatred for any other human being. Before long, all those would be gone, no longer part of our daily experience.

But how about those causes of depression for many, where they cannot point to any other person as being responsible for them? Boredom, unemployment, isolation, loneliness – these are apparently experienced by millions today. Will they still exist when we know that we and the material world around us are really spirit, with all that entails? Once we learn to manifest what we want to experience, plenty of good food for example, or a lovely home without a mortgage, will employment really matter? We'll need something to occupy us of course and keep us co-creating the world we experience, but no one will need to be employed to be happy. It's just something we might choose or not.

If you give it some thought, you'll probably come to the same conclusion I did, that there will be no need to experience loneliness and isolation unless we want to experience them (we'll still have free will to experience what we choose). When you know you are connected in that vast cosmic web of interconnections mentioned earlier, and that you can unite your consciousness with others, with plants and with animals, I'm guessing that very few of us would choose to ignore those connections and the loving, rewarding relationships they make possible. We'd send out loving feelings, attract abundance, amplify any love or abundance we attract, and send it out to others to use as they will. It's an endless circle of ever-expanding good times!

Realistic Subtitle?

In the subtitle of this book you'll see the claim that recognizing we are spirit, not matter, is at the heart of solving *all* the world's problems. Perhaps others can think of problems that will still exist, but I can't. As I see it, problems will be replaced by challenges.

We'll have the challenges of co-creating realities we'd like to experience, with the creation process limited to just ourselves if we choose or in collaboration with many other souls. We'll have a great number of choices and will need to decide among them and set some priorities, but I liken that to a kid in a candy store deciding which candy to eat first, or whether it might be better to create some new kind of candy that isn't in the store now. Not exactly what you'd classify as a problem.

It will be good times forever! Why would we decide to create problems? Better just to continually imagine new challenges, enjoy the thrill of new discoveries, and make contact with advanced intelligences that can help us enjoy the fun of unlimited creation and interaction that could lead us to new emotions and new levels of intensity in our enjoyment. We haven't begun to tap the number of forms we can inhabit, emotions we can experience, exuberant relationships we can enjoy and exciting worlds we can co-create.

As described in *The 2075 Movement,* the initial steps toward these developments will be under way by the year 2075. That's awfully close and I sure hope it comes about in the probable version of earth that I and those I love choose to experience, in the physical body or out of it.

But I'm not particularly concerned about it happening within a specific time frame, because after all, time doesn't really exist outside of our experiment. That means we can all be confident that right now, in some "future focus," we are already enjoying what is our "birthright" as the extremely powerful and loving beings we are at the soul level. And it will be all the more enjoyable for our having gone through the experiences of our "less than ideal" existences in our various incarnations here in HTSI.

About the Author

Dan McAneny spent 30 years compiling information for his first book on the afterlife, *You're Bigger Than Death ... and life too.* It presented evidence of credible communication from respected entities no longer in the physical body that emphasized our world is not what it seems, and that we are much more than we think we are. It also showed how these claims agreed with many of the conclusions and theories of quantum physicists. He later revised it under the title *You are Bigger than All Your Deaths.* In 2015 he realized there was an unimaginably positive message from one of the sources in his earlier book and decided to write a book about it. That book encourages a future version of him to become active in promoting the message. It is titled *The 2075 Movement.*

He followed that in 2016 with *Christ Was Not Crucified Thank God,* where he examined the closing days of the life of Jesus and its astounding implications as described by the entity Seth, channeled by Jane Roberts. In his next book, *We Are All Tourists,* he blended input from three major sources to share the perspective that all our lives, and all our existences in material form combined, are just a tiny fraction of who we are – spirits engaged primarily in non-material realities. He also addressed what that means for us. In 2017 he wrote *The Only 5 Things You Need to Know,* explaining how easy it is to become much happier if you know just five things.

In this book, published in 2018, *It's Spirit, Stupid, Not Matter,* Dan explores how much more advanced we might be as a civilization if we decided to seek out and follow advice and guidance from "dead people," spirits who lived just like us living spirits still in body, who have left behind the bonds and limits we take on when we enter a physical body at birth, and therefore have access to knowledge many levels of magnitude greater than ours.

Dan has also written a book on the promise of nanosilver for fighting infections, and two books for people on disability who want to start a business or get a job. He continues to work as an independent contractor for disability insurance companies, developing business plans for those referred to him. He previously worked in business consulting, outplacement, advertising, banking, manufacturing and sales. Dan and his wife Pat have lived in New Jersey, Virginia and North Carolina. They currently live in the Sarasota FL area. Their five children and several grandchildren live in various parts of the United States.

If you would like to order any of Dan's books on Amazon, all those published since 2015 list Dan McAneny as author, while his first book on the afterlife and its updated version list Daniel Thomas McAneny as author.